WILLIAM HENRY HARRISON
1773-1841

JOHN TYLER
1790-1862

Chronology—Documents—Bibliographical Aids

Edited by
DAVID A. DURFEE

Series Editor
HOWARD F. BREMER

Oceana Publications, Inc.
Dobbs Ferry, New York 10522

1970

Library of Congress Catalog Card Number: 76-116058
International Standard Book Number: 0-379-12081-X

PRINTED IN THE UNITED STATES OF AMERICA

TABLE OF CONTENTS

BIBLIOGRAPHICAL AIDS - John Tyler

EDITOR'S FOREWORD

Every attempt has been made to cite the most accurate dates in Chronology. Diaries, documents, and similar evidence have been used to determine the exact date. If, however, later scholarship has found such dates to be obviously erroneous, the more plausible date has been used.

This is a research tool compiled primarily for the student. While it does make some judgments on the significance of the events, it is hoped that they are reasoned judgments based on a long acquaintance with American History.

Obviously, the very selection of events by any writer is itself a judgment.

The essence of these books is in their making available some pertinent facts, providing some key documents, and adding a selective, critical bibliography which should direct the student to investigate additional and perhaps contradictory material for himself. Every effort has been made to cite the best of recent scholarship and, except for classics, to omit old, out of print works.

The emphasis in these volumes is on the period in which the individual actually served as President. This cannot be done in the case of William Henry Harrison, however, since he served in that office for only one month. Documents have been selected, therefore, which shed light on his qualifications for the office, the sources of his popularity and his attitude toward the Presidency.

Documents in this volume are taken from American State Papers, Indian Affairs, Volume I, Remarks of General Harrison Late Envoy Extraordinary and Minister Plenipotentiary of the United States to the Republic of Colombia (Washington, D.C., 1830), and James D. Richardson, ed., Messages and Papers of the Presidents, Vol. IV (Washington, D.C., 1897).

WILLIAM HENRY HARRISON
1773-1841

CHRONOLOGY

WILLIAM HENRY HARRISON

NINTH PRESIDENT OF THE UNITED STATES

EARLY LIFE

1773

July 12   Born on one of family estates, Berkeley Hundred, Virginia, the seventh and youngest child of Benjamin Harrison V and Elizabeth Bassett Harrison. The family's ancestry in America went back to Benjamin Harryson who was Clerk of the Virginia Council in 1632.

1776

July 4   Benjamin Harrison V, a representative to the Continental Congress from Virginia, having supported Lee's motion for independence July 2, voted for adoption of the Declaration of Independence. Signed the document when it had been engrossed.

1781

January 4   British forces under Benedict Arnold active in Virginia. Berkeley Hundred mansion stripped of all valuables by Arnold's forces.

1787

Entered Hampden Sidney College in Prince Edward County, Virginia, to prepare for the study of medicine.

1790

Moved to Richmond to work in the office of Dr. Andrew Leiper. In Richmond he joined the anti-slavery Humane Society, a membership which was later to embarrass him with southern voters.

1791

Entered Medical School of Pennsylvania University at Philadelphia to continue studies.

April 4	Benjamin Harrison V died. Robert Morris, the financier, appointed guardian of William Henry who inherited 3,000 acres. John Tyler, father of the future successor of William Henry, succeeded to Benjamin V's seat in the House of Burgesses.
August 16	Received commission as Ensign in the First United States Regiment of Infantry. Began service as a recruiting officer in Philadelphia.
Spetember 20	Departed from Philadelphia in command of 80 men for service at Fort Washington which defended Cincinnati.

1793

March	Exchanged inherited land in Virginia for 1,500 pounds and land in Kentucky from brother Benjamin VI.

1794

August 20	Served as Third Aide-de-Camp to General Anthony Wayne in the Battle of Fallen Timbers. Was active in carrying orders to areas where action was hottest. Cited for performance under fire. Patterned later military tactics after those of Wayne.

1795

November 25	Married Anna Tuthill Symmes, daughter of Ohio judge, John Cleves Symmes despite her father's objections to the match. Judge later became reconciled and the two men enjoyed friendly relations.

1796

Spring	Placed in command of Fort Washington by General Wilkinson.
September 29	Daughter, Betsy Bassett, born.

1797

Made home with wife on newly purchased 160 acre farm at North Bend, near Cincinnati, living in later famous "Log Cabin." Continued in command of Fort Washington but involved in local business including purchase of distillery.

Summer	Received Captain's commission.

1798

June 1   Resigned from army upon being appointed Land Of-
                fice Register.

June 28   Appointed Secretary of the Northwest Territory.

October   Son, John Cleves Symmes, born.

CONGRESSIONAL DELEGATE AND
TERRITORIAL GOVERNOR

1799

December 16   Seated as Territorial Delegate to Congress from
                the Northwest Territory following election as a
                Republican and supporter of liberalized provisions
                for purchasing western lands.

1800

March 31   Bill, which he had introduced, to divide the North-
                west Territory into two parts, passed by Congress.
                Nominated as Governor of the western part, the
                Indiana Territory, by President John Adams.

April 2   "Harrison Land Law," allowing one half of all
                public land to be sold in half-section lots, passed.
                Harrison had sponsored and worked for this to make
                it possible for men of lesser means to own land.

Spetember   Daughter, Lucy Singleton, born.

1801

January 10   Sworn in as Governor in the territorial capital at
                Vincennes.

1802

September   Negotiated treaty gaining cession of land by Miami
                and Delaware Indians. Signed September 17.

September 6   Son, William Henry, Jr., born.

December   Presided over convention at Vincennes which led to
                petition to Congress, submitted March 2, 1803, for
                a ten year suspension of the prohibition against
                slavery in the Indiana Territory.

1803

Summer   Negotiated treaty with Kaskaskias gaining cession
                of land.

1804

March 26   District of Louisiana joined to Indiana for adminis-
                trative purposes (until July 4, 1805). Harrison com-
                plained about the additional duties without additional
                emoluments.

Fall   Negotiated treaties with Sacs and Foxes and with
                Delawares and Piankeshaws gaining cessions of land.
                Treaties submitted to the Senate by President Jef-
                ferson November 30.

October 4   Son, John Scott, born.

1805

July 29   Delivered first Annual Message to the Indiana Gen-
                eral Assembly.

August 21   Completed negotiations of treaties with Piankeshaws
                and with Miamis, Delawares and Potawatomies gain-
                ing cessions of land.

1806

June 16   Eclipse predicted by The Prophet, Shawnee leader
                and brother of Tecumsah, convinced many Indians of
                his power. This increased the amount of support for
                his movement to purge Indian areas of white influ-
                ence and resist white occupation of lands ceded in
                treaties.

                Son, Benjamin, born.

                Visited at his Vincennes home, Grouselands, by
                Aaron Burr while Burr was developing plans which
                eventually led to his trial for treason.

1807-1808

Continued as Governor of Indiana Territory. Movement to divide Territory into two parts, Indiana and
Illinois, developed. Harrison opposed the division on
the grounds that it was desired only by land specula-
tors and that it would lead to too rapid expansion into new areas and bring on conflict with the Indian
tribes. Supporters of separation gained strength and
in 1808 were able to elect Jesse B. Thomas, an oppon-

ent of Harrison, as Indiana Territorial Delegate to Congress.

1809

January 22   Daughter, Mary Symmes, born.

February 3   Bill to divide Illinois from Indiana, opposed by Harrison, passed by Congress.

May   Harrison supported candidate defeated by Jonathan Jennings, "candidate of the people," in popular election for delegate to Congress.

September 30   Treaty of Fort Wayne, gaining cession of vast areas from Miamis, Delawares, Potawatomies, Weas and Eel Rivers, signed after negotiation with assemblage of over 1,000 Indians.

Negotiated treaty gaining cession of land with Kickapoos.

1810

Continued conflict with land speculator critics with charges and countercharges exchanged. Increased tension in relations with Indians.

1811

April   Instituted lawsuit for $9,000 against William McIntosh on charges that he had slandered Harrison by spreading rumors that he had profitted personally at the expense of the Indians in his dealings with them. Awarded $4,000 in damages.

July 27   Visited at Vincennes by Tecumsah who, with The Prophet, had been organizing northern tribes to resist takeover of land ceded in the Treaty of Fort Wayne. No positive results from council.

September 26   Left Vincennes for Prophetstown in command of army reinforced by newly arrived Fourth Regiment of regular United States infantry.

October 26   Son, Carter Bassett, born.

November 7   Encamped with army of approximately 1,000 men on Burnet's Creek near Prophetstown and the Tippecanoe River. Camp attacked by slightly smaller

Indian force, many of whom had been convinced by The Prophet that bullets would not be able to harm them. Attack repelled with high casualties on each side. Disillusioned Indians turned on The Prophet. Prophetstown abandonned. Sacked and burned by Harrison's army the following day.

November 18   Returned to Vincennes.

1812

April   Despite scattered outbreaks and Harrison's opposition, Fourth Regiment ordered to return to Ohio. Harrison sent family to Ohio via Kentucky for safety.

GENERAL IN THE WAR OF 1812

June 18   War declared by Congress.

June 19   Left for tour of Kentucky enroute to rejoining his family at Cincinnati. Gained political support and backing for position of military leadership in Kentucky, especially from Governor Shelby.

August 22   Commissioned a brigadier general by President Madison.

August 25   Appointed a major general in the Kentucky militia.

August 29   Departed for relief of Fort Wayne having assumed command of the Northwestern Army consisting of four regiments, the regular army Seventeenth and three of Kentucky militia. The army had originally been gathered to relieve General Hull at Fort Dearborn. Hull's surrender had made the army available for this use.

September 18   Succeeded by General Winchester as commander of the Northwestern Army when orders from the War Department failed to assign the command to Harrison. Winchester's regular army commission was senior to that of Harrison and the latter's Kentucky commission as a major general could not give him the command without specific instructions from Washington.

September 24   Received appointment to replace Winchester in command of the army.

December 28   Resigned as governor of Indiana Territory.

1813

January 22   Winchester, in command of advance forces, having
                   moved to exposed position on the Raisin River (just
                   north of the border between Ohio and Michigan), cap-
                   tured. Agreed to surrender of forces under his com-
                   mand while in British custody. Later killed by Indian
                   allies of British. Critics of Harrison later accused
                   him of ordering Winchester to move into dangerous
                   territory and then failing to support him. Most serious
                   detractors implied that it was done purposely to elim-
                   inate a rival for command.

April 28   Harrison and main force besieged at Fort Meigs.
                   Saved from destruction by artillery by the construc-
                   tion of giant earth redoubt. Siege lifted May 7.

Summer   Spent summer seeking sailors and supplies and await-
                   ing the clearing of the British fleet from Lake Erie
                   before he could move into Detroit or Canada.

September 10   Ships under Commodore Oliver H. Perry defeated
                   Commodore Barclay's British fleet on Lake Erie.

September 27   General Proctor abandonned endangered British
                   strong points at Fort Amherstburg and Malden and
                   began retreat up Thames River.

September 30   Harrison's forces reoccupied Detroit.

October 5   Defeated Proctor's army at Battle of the Thames.
                   Proctor retreated, Tecumsah was killed. More than
                   600 British troops taken prisoner. Harrison did not
                   pursue the defeated enemy but, instead, returned
                   with his forces to United States territory. Critics
                   blamed him for not following up his victory.

October 28   Daughter, Anna Tuthill, born.

Winter   On orders moved army to the eastern end of Lake
                   Erie and awaited orders to move. The army received
                   no such orders and remained idle.

May 11   Submitted resignation as major general after he
                   failed to receive appointment as lieutenant general
                   and after Secretary of War John Armstrong sent
                   orders directly to his subordinates rather than

sending them through Harrison. Convinced that Secretary's actions were the result of political rivalry between New Yorker Armstrong and his predecessor as Secretary of War, Monroe, both presidential aspirants.

May 28   Vacancy in ranks of major generals caused by Harrison's resignation filled by appointment of Andrew Jackson.

After brief stay in the East and visit to Washington Harrison returned to North Bend. Original "Log Cabin" at North Bend enlarged to a total of 16 rooms.

IN STATE AND NATIONAL OFFICES

1815

August 25   Served as chief commissioner in arranging a peace treaty with nine Indian tribes at Spring Wells near Detroit. Treaty signed September 8.

Son, James Findlay, born.

December 20   Requested an official investigation into his conduct as a general by the House of Representatives following renewal of charges of profiteering in purchase of supplies. Select committee headed by Richard M. Johnson appointed.

1816

October   Elected to Congress for incompleted term and full term until March, 1819. Campaigned on issues of militia reorganization, relief for needy veterans and repeal of the recently passed Compensation Law which had increased congressional salaries. Received some Federalist as well as Republican support.

December 2   Entered House. John Tyler, also elected to fill an incomplete term, entered at same time.

1817

January 23   Johnson Committee report cleared Harrison of improper behavior in obtaining supplies.

1818

February   Supported censure of Jackson's venture into Florida.

March 30   Received belated vote of thanks from Congress. His
                        name and that of Governor Shelby of Kentucky had
                        been deleted from the resolution adopted at the con-
                        clusion of the War of 1812 because of the charges
                        against Harrison.

November 23   Declared his opposition both to slavery and to federal
                        laws to prohibit it. Stated that he would abhor its
                        introduction into the Northwest Territory but that
                        states in that area should not be bound by an ordin-
                        ance they had never consented to.

1819-1820

Deciding against running for reelection to Congress
he returned to North Bend. In addition to farming he
reentered the State Senate and served as a director
of the Cincinnati branch of the Bank of the United
States. Because of his opposition to the Bank he was
accused, at best, of inconsistency.

1821

Although supported by the pro-southern members of
the legislature Harrison lost a bid for selection as
United States Senator from Ohio.

1822-1823

Defeated by William Gazley in attempt to regain
House seat. Beset by financial difficulties and attacks by critics of his war record.

1824

Requested appointment as minister to Mexico. Failed
to receive the mission.

Summer   Supported Clay's successful campaign in Ohio.

1825-1827

Harrison served in the United States Senate to which
he was chosen in February, 1825, in spite of a series
of attacks on his character by opponents. Was Chair-
man of the military and militia committees. He supported the President on questions of internal improvements. Daughter, Lucy Singleton, died April 7, 1826.

1828

January 4   Treasury Secretary Richard Rush nominated as run-
             ning mate for Adams as a result of Clay's efforts.
             Harrison had received som encouragement to believe
             he might gain the nomination to counter the appeal of
             Jackson's military record.

May 22   Nominated as Minister to Colombia. Had sought such
             appointment, largely for financial reasons, since
             1824.

1829

February 5   Arrived in Bogota with instructions to encourage
             republican opposition to the development of a dicta-
             torship by Bolivar but without interfering in the
             internal affairs of Colombia.

March 11   Thomas Patrick Moore named by President Jackson
             to replace Harrison. Harrison asked to continue un-
             til Moore's arrival in September.

September 27 Sent letter to Bolivar as one general to another point-
             ing out the benefits that would come both to him and
             to Colombia if he would reject the advice of those
             advocating a dictatorship and the disaster that would
             overtake him if he accepted that advice.

RETURN TO PRIVATE LIFE

1830

January   Departed from Colombia after being accused of
             participating in anti-Bolivar plot of General Cordova.
             Harrison later became convinced that suspicions had
             been planted by political enemies including his suc-
             cessor, Moore. Prepared a defense of his actions.

April 15   Arrived in Cincinnati to face continuing financial
             problems. Difficulties compounded by family trou-
             bles. Son William's experience led him to give up
             alcoholic beverages including hard cider. John Cleves
             Symmes, his oldest son, had been removed from his
             position as head of the Vincennes Land Office by
             Jackson and was being held liable for disputed Land
             Office claims.

October 30   Son, John Cleves Symmes, died.

1831-1832

Devoted most of his energies to running the farm
and attempting to repair his financial position dam-
aged by his accepting responsibility for the unpaid
debts of his sons William and Symmes and of Cincinnati friends. Floods in the spring of 1832 also
hurt. To meet obligations he sold much of the farming land he had earlier acquired. He also suffered
several illnesses during these years. He kept in
touch with political associates and supported Clay
against Jackson in 1832.

1833

February 13   Wrote to Lewis Cass supporting Jackson's rejection of the idea of nullification and Force Bill.

July 4   Gave oration a Cheviot, Ohio, calling for improved
relations between the North and South and opposing
nullification on the one side and abolitionism and
emancipation through colonization on the other.

August 20   Grandson, Benjamin, future President, born. Child of
John Scott Harrison.

1834

October   Named Clerk of the County Court of Common Pleas
in Cincinnati as a means of improving his financial
condition.

1835

January 9   Whig and Anti-Mason convention meeting in Harrisburg, Pennsylvania, recommended Harrison for the
presidency. Followed by organization of "Tippecanoe Clubs" which celebrated anniversary dates or
Harrison victories and sought to refute continuing
atticks on his military record. Most of these attacks
in recent months had been designed to promote the
cause of Col. Richard M. Johnson who had served
under him at the Thames. Harrison, not having either
a state or federal government office which would
provide him an opportunity to express his views,
did so in occasional speeches and frequent letters.

April 22   Took a moderate position on the issue of Masonry
stating that he was no Mason but that he would not
take action against that organization. Also opposed

excessive presidential power and the spoils system.

August

Headed a three state committee in an unsuccessful effort to promote a railroad between the Ohio Valley and South Carolina.

December 16

Nominated for president by Whig and Anti-Mason convention in Pennsylvania. Later gained nominations in Delaware, Indiana, Maryland and Ohio but lost in Virginia. William P. Magnum of North Carolina, Daniel Webster of Massachusetts and Hugh L. White of Tennessee were other regional candidates of Whigs in their attempt to throw the election into the House.

1836

May 1

Sent letter outlining his positions on distribution, internal improvements, the Bank and expunction for publication in "Niles' Weekly Register."

September 14

Harrison arrived in Richmond on the one major trip of the campaign period. For the most part he had remained at home in North Bend and received visitors but felt this trip necessary to counter rumors of ill health.

December 7

Received total of 73 electoral votes to 170 for the victorious Van Buren. Carried Deleware, Indiana, Kentucky, Maryland, New Jersey, Ohio and Vermont.

1837

Year spent on farm at North Bend. Supporters of Clay, Harrison and Webster, the three leading contenders for 1840, maneuvered for position.

1838

February 6

Son, William Henry, died.

May

Ohio Whig convention declared unanimously for Harrison and called for a national convention. Whig Congressional caucus also called for such a convention to meet in December, 1839.

July 4

Spoke in Massillon, Ohio, as part of a speaking tour in parts of Ohio that were Clay territory.

November	Nominated for president by the Democratic Anti-Masonic National Convention.

1839

June 12	Webster, in London, facing opposition in his home state led by Edward Everett, withdrew from the contest for the Whig nomination.
August 12	Thurlow Weed of New York, chief developer of the coalition to prevent Clay's nomination, visited Clay at Saratoga, N.Y. and attempted unsuccessfully to convince him he too should withdraw. Harrison's son, Carter Bassett, died.
December 4	Democratic Whig National Convention convened in Harrisburg. Largest number of delegates behind Clay but Weed headed a large block of supporters of General Winfield Scott and Thadeus Stevens of Pennsylvania similar bloc for Harrison. Weed pushed through a unit rule which hurt Clay's chances.
December 6	Following revelation by Stevens of a Scott letter appearing to court anti-slavery support, Virginia shifted from Clay to Harrison to prevent a possible Scott victory. Harrison nominated by 148 votes to 90 for Clay and 16 for Scott. Tyler named for vice-presidency in attempt by Weed and Stevens to appease Clay forces. Angered, the Clay supporters prevented adoption of a platform.

1840

June 11	Attended Fort Meigs reunion celebration to end talk of illness. One of few appearances in campaign in a summer marked by death of son, Benjamin (June 9) and illness of wife, Anna. Supporters campaigned for him as the log cabin and hard cider candidate (in spite of the fact that his "Log Cabin" had 16 rooms and that he had given up hard cider and other alcoholic beverages ten years earlier.
November 10	Carried states with a total of 234 electoral votes. Van Buren and Johnson received 60.
December 2	Electoral College met.

1841

February 9   Arrived in Washington and conducted negotiations for cabinet and other positions.

PRESIDENT

March 4   William Henry Harrison inaugurated as ninth President. Cabinet, after Clay had refused the State Department, included: Daniel Webster of Massachusetts, Secretary of State; Thomas Ewing of Ohio, Secretary of the Treasury; John Bell of Tennessee, Secretary of War; John J. Crittenden of Kentucky, Attorney General; Francis Granger of New York, Postmaster General; George Badger of North Carolina, Secretary of the Navy.

March 13   Rebuffed Clay's attempt to get him to call an immediate special session of Congress to deal with financial issues. Feeling slighted, Clay left Washington. After Clay's departure Harrison called session for May 31.

March 27   Walked in slush and became ill.

April 4   Died 12:30 A.M. after only one month in office. Webster sent his own son to notify John Tyler.

April 7   Funeral held. Buried in Washington. Body removed to North Bend in June.

REPORT OF THE BATTLE OF TIPPECANOE
November 18, 1811

*The campaign to make William Henry Harrison a candidate
for the presidency and then to elect him was based largely
on his reputation as a military hero, as the victor in the
battles of Tippecanoe and the Thames. The reputation
was not unchallenged. Others claimed credit for the victories and especially in the case of Tippecanoe accused
Harrison of having to fight a desperate battle and sustain
heavy losses because he had left his forces unnecessarily
vulnerable to attack.*

*Harrison's own official report on this battle, explaining
and defending his actions to the Secretary of War, was
prepared and dispatched upon his return to his territorial
capital at Vincennes, Indiana.*

Vincennes, 18th November, 1811

Sir:

In my letter of the 8th instant, I did myself the honor to communicate the result of an action between the troops under my command
and the confederation of Indians under the control of the Shawanese
prophet. I had previously informed you, in a letter of the 2d instant,
of my proceedings previously to my arrival at the Vermillion river,
where I had erected a block house for the protection of the boats
which I was obliged to leave, and as a depository for our heavy baggage, and such part of our provisions as we were unable to transport
in wagons.

On the morning of the 3d instant, I commenced my march from the
block house. The Wabash, above this, turning considerably to the east-
ward, I was obliged, in order to avoid the broken and woody country,
which borders upon it, to change my course to the westward of north
to gain the prairies which lie to the back of those woods. At the end of
one day's march, I was enabled to take the proper direction, (N.E.),
which brought me, on the evening of the 5th, to a small creek, at about
eleven miles from the Prophet's town. I had, on the preceeding day,
avoided the dangerous pass of Pine creek, by inclining a few miles to
the left, where the troops and wagons were crossed with expedition

15

and safety. Our route on the 6th, for about six miles, lay through prairies, separated by small points of woods.

My order of march hitherto had been similar to that used by General Wayne; that is, the infantry were in two columns of files on either side of the road, and the mounted riflemen and cavalry in front, in the rear, and on the flanks. Where the ground was unfavorable for the action of cavalry, they were placed on the rear, but where it was otherwise, they were made to exchange positions with one of the mounted rifle corps. Understanding that the last four miles were open woods, and the probability being greater that we should be attacked in front than on either flank, I halted at that distance from the town, and formed the army in order of battle. The U.S. infantry placed in the centre, two companies of militia infantry, and one of mounted riflemen, on each flank, formed the front line. In the rear of this line was placed the baggage, drawn up as compactly as possible, and immediately behind it a reserve of three companies of militia infantry. The cavalry formed a second line, at the distance of three hundred yards in the rear of the front line, and a company of mounted riflemen the advanced guard at that distance in front. To facilitate the march, the whole were then broken off in short columns of companies – a situation the most favorable for forming in order of battle with facility and precision.

Our march was slow and cautious, and much delayed by the examination of every place which seemed calculated for an ambuscade. Indeed, the ground was, for some time, so unfavorable, that I was obliged to change the position of the several corps three times in the distance of a mile. At half past two o'clock, we passed a small creek at the distance of one mile and a half from the town, and entered an open wood, when the army was halted, and again drawn up in order of battle. During the whole of the last day's march, parties of Indians were constantly about us, and every effort was made by the interpreters to speak to them, but in vain. New attempts of the kind were now made, but, proving quite ineffectual, a Capt. Dubois, of the spies and guides, offering to go with a flag to the town, I despatched him, with an interpreter, to request a conference with the Prophet. In a few moments a messenger was sent by Captain Dubois to inform me that, in his attempts to advance, the Indians appeared on both his flanks, and although he had spoken to them in a most friendly manner, they refused to answer, but beckoned to him to go forward, and constantly endeavored to cut him off from the army. Upon this information, I recalled the Captain, and determined to encamp for the night, and take some other measures for opening a conference with the Prophet.

Whilst I was engaged in tracing the lines for the encompment, Major Daviess, who commanded the dragoons, came to inform me that he had penetrated to the Indian fields; that the ground was entirely open and favorable; that the Indians in front had manifested nothing but hostility, and had answered every attempt to bring them to a parley, with contempt and insolence. I was immediately advised by all the officers around me to move forward; a similar wish indeed pervaded all the army. It was drawn up in excellent order, and every man appeared eager to decide the contest immediately.

Being informed that a good encampment might be had upon the Wabash, I yielded to what appeared the general wish, and directed the troops to advance, taking care, however, to place the interpreters in front, with directions to invite a conference with any Indians they might meet with. We had not advanced above four hundred yards when I was informed that three Indians had approached the advanced guard, and had expressed a wish to speak to me. I found, upon their arrival, that one of them was a man in great estimation with the Prophet. He informed me that the chiefs were much surprised at my advancing upon them so rapidly; that they were given to understand, by the Delewares and Miamies, whom I had sent to them a few days before, that I would not advance to their town until I had received an answer to my demands made through them; that this answer had been despatched by the Pottawatamy Chief, Winnemae, who had accompanied the Miamies and Delewares on their return; that they had left the Prophet's town two days before, with a design to meet me, but had unfortunately taken the road on the south side of the Wabash. I answered that I had no intention of attacking them, until I discovered that they would not comply with the demands that I had made; that I would go on and encamp at the Wabash; and in the morning would have an interview with the Prophet and his chiefs, and explain to them the determination of the President; that, in the mean time, no hostilities should be committed.

He seemed much pleased with this, and promised that it should be observed on their parts. I then resumed my march. We struck the cultivated ground about five hundred yards below the town, but as these extended to the bank of the Wabash, there was no possibility of getting an encampment which was provided with both wood and water.

My guides and interpreters still being with the advanced guard, and taking the direction of the town, the army followed, and had advanced within about one hundred and fifty yards, when fifty or sixty Indians sallied out, and, with loud acclamations called to the cavalry and to the infantry, which were on our right flank, to halt. I immediately advanced to the front, caused the army to halt, and directed an interpreter to request some of the chiefs to come to me. In a few moments the man who had been with me before, made his appearance. I informed him that my object, for the present, was to procure a good piece of ground to encamp on, where we could get wood and water. He informed me that there was a creek to the northwest which he thought would suit our purpose. I immediately despatched two officers to examine it, and they reported that the situation was excellent. I then took leave of the chief, and a mutual promise was again made for suspension of hostilities until we could have an interview on the following day. I found the ground destined for the encampment not altogether such as I would wish it. It was, indeed, admirably calculated for the encampment of regular troops that were opposed to regulars, but it afforded great facility to the approach of savages. It was a piece of dry oak land, rising about ten feet above the level of a marshy prairie in front, (towards the Indian town) and nearly twice that height above a similar prairie in the rear, through which, and near to this bank, ran a small stream clothed with willows and brush wood. Towards the left flank this bench of high land widened considerably, but became gradually narrower in the opposite direction, and at the distance of one hundred and fifty yards from the right flank terminated in an abrupt point. The two columns of infantry occupied the front and rear of this ground, at the distance of about one hundred and fifty yards from each other on the left, and something more than half that distance on the right flank. These flanks were filled up, the first by two companies of mounted riflemen, amounting to about one hundred and twenty men, under the command of Major General Wells, of the Kentucky militia, who served as a major, the other by Spencer's company of mounted riflemen, which amounted to eighty men. The front line was composed of one battalion of United States' infantry under the command of Major Floyd, flanked on the right by two companies of militia, and on the left by one company. The rear line was composed of a battalion of United States' troops, under the command of Captain Baen, acting as major, and four companies of militia infantry under Lieutenant Colonel Decker.

The regular troops of this line joined the mounted riflemen, under General Wells on the left flank, and Colonel Decker's battalion formed an angle with Spencer's company on the left.

Two troops of dragoons, amounting to, in aggregate, about sixty men, were encamped in the rear of the left flank, and Captain Parke's troop, which was larger than the other two, in the rear of the front line. Our order of encampment varied little from that above described, excepting when some peculiarity of the ground made it necessary. For a night attack, the order of encampment was the order of battle, and each man slept immediately opposite to his post in the line. In the formation of my troops I used a single rank, or what is called Indian file; because, in Indian warfare, where there is no shock to resist, one rank is nearly as good as two, and in that kind of warfare, the extension of line is a matter of first importance. Raw troops also manoeuvre with much more facility in single than in double ranks. It was my constant custom to assemble all the field officers at my tent, every evening, by signal, to give them the watch-word, and their instructions for the night; those given for the night of the 6th were, that each corps which formed a part of the exterior line of the encampment should hold its own ground until relieved. The dragoons were directed to parade dismounted, in case of a night attack, with their pistols in their belts, and to act as a corps de reserve. The camp was defended by two captain's guards, consisting each of four non-commissioned officers and forty-two privates, and two subaltern's guards of twenty non-commissioned officers and privates. The whole under the command of a field officer of the day.

The troops were regularly called up, an hour before day, and made to continue under arms until it was quite light. On the morning of the 7th, I had risen a quarter after 4 o'clock, and the signal for calling out the men would have been given in two minutes, when the attack commenced. It began on our left flank; but a single gun was fired by the sentinels or by the guard in that direction, which made not the least resistance, but abandonned their officer and fled into camp, and the first notice which the troops of that flank had of the danger was from the yells of the savages within a short distance of the line; but, even under those circumstances, the men were not wanting to themselves or to the occasion. Such of them as were awake, or were easily awakened, seized their arms, and took their stations, others, which were more tardy, had to contend with the enemy in the doors of their tents. The storm first fell upon Captain Barton's company, of the 4th United States' regiment, and Captain Geiger's company of mounted riflemen, which formed the left angle of the rear line. The fire upon these was excessively severe, and they suffered considerably before relief could be brought to them. Some few Indians passed into the encampment near the angle, and one or two penetrated to some distance, before they were killed. I believe all other companies were under arms and tolerably formed before they were fired on. The morning was dark and cloudy. Our fires afforded partial light, which, if it gave us some opportunity of taking our positions, was still more advantageous to the enemy, affording them the means of taking a surer aim; they were, therefore, extinguished as soon as possible. Under all these discouraging circumstances, the troops (nineteen-twentieths of whom had never been in action before) behaved in a manner that can never be too much applauded. They took their places without noise, and with less confusion than could have been expected from veterans, placed in a similar situation. As soon as I could mount my horse, I rode to the angle that was attacked. I found that Barton's company had suffered severely, and the left of Geiger's entirely broken. I immediately ordered Cook's company, and the late Captain Wentworth's, under Lieutenant Peters, to be brought up from the centre of the rear line, where the ground was much more defensible, and formed across the angle in support of Barton's and Geiger's. My attention was then engaged by a heavy firing upon the left of the front line, where were stationed the small company of United States' riflemen, (then, however, armed with muskets) and the companies of Baen, Snelling, and Prescott, of the 4th regiment. I found Major Daviess forming the dragoons in the rear of those companies; and understanding that the heaviest part of the enemy's fire proceeded from some trees about fifteen or twenty paces in front of those companies, I directed the Major to dislodge them with a part of the dragoons; unfortunately, the major's gallantry determined him to execute the order with a smaller force than was sufficient, which enabled the enemy to avoid him in front, and attack his flanks. The major was mortally wounded, and his party driven back. The Indians were, however, immediately and gallantly dislodged from their advantageous position by Captain Snelling, at the head of his company. In the course of a few minutes after the commencement of the attack, the fire extended along the left flank, the whole of the front, the right flank, and part of the rear line. Upon Spencer's mounted riflemen and the right of Warwick's company, which was posted on the right of the rear line, it was excessively severe. Captain Spencer, and his first and second lieutenants, were killed, and Captain Warwick mortally wounded. Those companies, however, still bravely maintained their posts, but Spencer had suffered so severely, and having originally too much ground to occupy, I reinforced them with Robb's company of riflemen, which had been drawn, or, by mistake, ordered from their position on the left flank, towards the centre of the camp, and filled the vacancy that had been occupied by Robb, with Prescott's company of the 4th United States' regiment. My great object was to keep the lines entire, to prevent the enemy from breaking into the camp, until day-light should enable me to make a general and effectual charge. With this view, I had reinforced every part of the line that had suffered much, and as soon as the approach of morning had discovered itself, I withdrew from the front line Snelling's, Posey's, (under Lieutenant Albright) and Scott's, and from the rear line, Wilson's companies, and drew them up upon the left flank, and, at the same time, I ordered Cook's and Baen's companies, the former from the rear, and the latter from the front line, to reinforce the right flank, foreseeing that, at these points, the enemy would make their last efforts. Major Wells, who commanded on the left flank, not knowing my intentions precisely, had taken the command of these companies, and had charged the enemy before I had formed the body of dragoons, with which I meant to support the infantry; a small detachment of these were, however, ready and proved amply sufficient for the purpose.

The Indians were driven by the infantry at the point of the bayonet, and the dragoons pursued and forced them into a marsh, where they could not be followed. Captain Cook and Lieutenant Larabee had, agreeably to my order, marched their companies to the right flank; had formed them under the fire of the enemy, and, being then joined by the riflemen of that flank, had charged the Indians, killed a number, and put the rest to precipitate flight. A favorable opportunity was here offered to pursue the enemy with dragoons, but being engaged at that time on the other flank, I did not observe it until it was too late.

I have thus, sir, given you the particulars of an action which was certainly maintained with the greatest obstinacy and perseverance by both parties. The Indians manifested a ferocity, uncommon even with them. To their savage fury, our troops opposed that cool and deliberate valor which is characteristic of the Christian soldier.

*   *   *   *

After mentioning those deserving special notice
and listing those killed in action, he continued:

All these gentlemen, sir, Captain Baen excepted, have left wives, and five of them, large families of children. This is the case, too, with many of the privates among the militia, who fell in the action, or who have died since, of their wounds.

Will the bounty of their country be withheld from their helpless orphans, many of whom will be in the most destitute condition, and, perhaps, even want the necessaries of life?

With respect to the number of Indians that were engaged against us, I am possessed of no data by which I can form a correct statement. It must, however, have been considerable, and perhaps not much inferior to our own, which, deducting the dragoons, who were unable to do us much service, was very little above seven hundred non-commissioned officers and privates. I am convinced there were, at least, six hundred. The Prophet had, three weeks before, four hundred and fifty of his own proper followers. I am induced to believe, that he was joined by a number of the lawless vagabonds who live on the Illinois river, as large trails were seen coming from that direction. Indeed, I shall not be surprised to find, that some of those who professed the warmest friendship for us, were arrayed against us. It is certain, that one of this description came out from the town, and spoke to me the night before the action....

LETTER TO SIMON BOLIVAR
Bogota, Colombia, September 27, 1829

Except for negotiations with Indians who had support from the British in Canada and his military operations in the War of 1812, Harrison's only experience in foreign relations before his election as President was his brief tenure as Minister to Colombia in 1829. His desire for the post was apparently based more on financial need than any long-standing interest in the affairs of Latin America. He was, however, concerned about the fate of republican government in that area and especially in Colombia where Bolivar, confronted by rebellion, was becoming more and more dictatorial.

Harrison's instructions to work for the preservation of the republican form without interfering in the internal affairs of Colombia would have been difficult for anyone to carry out. Harrison attempted to accomplish them through a direct appeal from one general to another. Before he left Colombia, Harrison was accused of involvement in plots against the government. He blamed this on treacherous actions by Americans on the ministry staff. His critics blamed it on his undiplomatic behavior as exemplified by the letter to Bolivar.

The letter also shows the fear of excessive executive power that was the foundation of his political ideas.

BOGOTA, 27th September, 1829

SIR: If there is any thing, in the style, the matter, or the object, of this letter, which is calculated to give offence to your Excellency, I am persuaded, you will readily forgive it, when you reflect on the motives which induced me to write it. An old soldier could possess no feelings but those of the kindest character, toward one who has shed so much lustre on the profession of arms; nor can a citizen of the country of Washington cease to wish that, in Bolivar, the world might behold another instance of the highest military attainments, united with the purest patriotism, and the greatest capacity for civil Government.

Such, sir, have been the fond hopes, not only of the People of the United States, but of the friends of liberty throughout the world. I will not say that your Excellency has formed projects to defeat these hopes. But, there is no doubt, that they have not only been formed, but are, at this moment, in progress to maturity, and openly avowed by those who possess your entire confidence. I will not attribute to these men impure motives; but can they be disinterested advisers? Are they not the very persons who will gain most by the proposed change? – who will, indeed, gain all that is to be gained, without furnishing any part of the equivalent? That that, the price of their future wealth and honors, is to be furnished exclusively by yourself? And of what does it consist? Your great character. Such a one, that, if a man were wise, and possessed of the Empire of the Caesars, in its best days, he would give all to obtain. Are you prepared to make this sacrifice, for such an object?

I am persuaded that those who advocate these measures, have never dared to induce you to adopt them, by any argument founded on your personal interests; and that, to succeed, it would be necessary to convince you that no other course remained, to save the country from the evils of anarchy. This is the question, then, to be examined.

Does the history of this country, since the adoption of the Constitution, really exhibit unequivocal evidence that the People are unfit to be free? Is the exploded opinion of a European Philosopher, of the last age, that, "in the new hemisphere, man is a degraded being," to be renewed, and supported by the example of Colombia? The proofs should, indeed, be strong, to induce an American to adopt an opinion so humiliating.

Feeling always a deep interest in the success of the Revolutions in the late Spanish America, I have never been an inattentive observer of events, pending, and posterior to the achievements of its Independence. In these events, I search, in vain, for a single fact to show that, in Colombia, at least, the state of society is unsuited to the adoption of a free Government. Will it be said that a free Government did exist, but, being found inadequate to the objects for which it had been instituted, it has been superceded by one of a different character, with the concurrence of the majority of the People?

It is the most difficult thing in the world for me to believe that a People in the possession of their rights, as freemen, would ever be willing to surrender them, and submit themselves to the will of a master. If any such instances are on record, the power thus transferred has been in a moment of extreme public danger, and, then, limited to a very short period. I do not think that it is by any means certain, that the majority of the French People, favored the elevation of Napoleon to the throne of France. But, if it were so, how different were the circumstances of that country, from those of Colombia, when the Constitution of Cucuta was overthrown. At the period of the elevation of Napoleon to the First Consulate, all the powers of Europe were the open or secret enemies of France – civil war raged within her borders; the hereditary king possessed many partisans in every province; the People continually betrayed by the factions which murdered and succeeded each other, had imbided a portion of their ferocity, and every town and village, witnessed the indiscriminate slaughter of both men and women, of all parties and principles. Does the history

of Colombia, since the expulsion of the Spaniards, present any parallel
to these scenes? Her frontiers have been never seriously menaced —
no civil war raged — not a partisan of the former Government was to
be found in the whole extent of her territory — no factions contended
with each other for the possession of power; the Executive Govern-
remained in the hands of those to whom it had been committed by the
People, in a fair election. In fact, no People ever passed from under
the yoke of a despotic Government, to the enjoyment of entire freedom, with less disposition to abuse their newly acquired power, than
those of Colombia. They submitted, indeed, to a continuance of some
of the most arbitrary and unjust features which distinguished the former Government. If there was any disposition, on the part of the great
mass of the People, to effect any change in the existing order of
things; if the Colombians act from the same motives and upon the same
principles which govern mankind elsewhere, and in all ages, they
would have desired to take from the Government a part of the power,
which, in their inexperience, they had confided to it. The monopoly of
certain articles of agricultural produce, and the oppressive duty of
the Alcavala, might have been tolerated, until the last of the tyrants
were driven from the country. But when peace was restored, when no
one enemy remained within its borders, it might reasonably have been
supposed that the People would have desired to abolish these remains
of arbitrary Government, and substitute for them some tax more
equal and accordant with Republican principles.

On the contrary, it is pretended, that they had become enamored
with these despotic measures, and so disgusted with the freedom they
did enjoy, that they were more than willing to commit their destinies
to the uncontrolled will of your Excellency. Let me assure you, sir,
that these assertions will gain no credit with the present generation,
or with posterity. They will demand the facts, which had induced a
People, by no means deficient in intelligence, so soon to abandon the
principles for which they had so gallantly fought, and tamely surrender that liberty, which had been obtained at the expense of so much
blood. And what facts can be produced? It cannot be said that life and
property were not as well protected, under the Republican Government, as they have ever been; nor that there existed any oppostion to
the Constitution and laws, too strong for the ordinary powers of the
Government to put down.

If the insurrection of General Paez, in Venezuela, is adduced, I
would ask, by what means was he reduced to obedience? Your Excellency, the legitimate head of the Republic, appeared, and, in a moment,
all opposition ceased, and Venezuela was restored to the Republic.
But, it is said, that this was effected by your personal influence, or
the dread of your military talents, and that, to keep General Paez,
and other ambitious chiefs, from dismembering the Republic, it was
necessary to invest your Excellency with the extraordinary powers you
possess. There would be some reason in this, if you had refused to

act without these powers; or, having acted, as you did, you had been unable to accomplish anything without them. But you succeeded, completely, and there can be no possible reason assigned, why you would not have succeeded, with the same means, against any future attempt of General Paez, or any other General.

There appears, however, to be one sentiment, in which all parties unite; that is, that, as matters now stand, you alone can save the country from ruin, at least, from much calamity. They differ, however, very widely, as to the measures to be taken to put your Excellency in the way to render this important service. The lesser, and more interested party, is for placing the Government in your hands for life; either with your present title, or with one which, it must be confessed, better accords with the nature of the powers to be exercised. If they adopt the less offensive title, and if they weave into their system some apparent checks to your will, it is only for the purpose of masking, in some degree, their real object; which is nothing short of the establishment of a despotism. The plea of necessity, that eternal argument of all conspirators, ancient or modern, against the rights of mankind, will be resorted to, to induce you to accede to their measures; and the unsettled state of the country, which has been designedly produced by them, will be adduced as evidence of that necessity.

There is but one way for your Excellency to escape from the snares which have been so artfully laid to trap you, and that is, to stop short in the course which, unfortunately, has been already commenced. Every step you advance, under the influence of such councils, will make retreat more difficult, until it will become impracticable. You will be told that the intention is only to vest you with authority to correct what is wrong in the Administration, and to put down the factions, and that, when the country once enjoys tranquility, the Government may be restored to the People. Delusive will be the hopes of those who rely upon this declaration. The promised hour of tranquility will never arrive. If events tended to produce it, they would be counteracted by the Government itself. It was the strong remark of a former President of the United States, that, "Sooner will the lover be contented with the first smiles of his mistress, than a Government cease to endeavor to preserve and extend its powers." With whatever reluctance your Excellency may commence the career; with whatever disposition to abandon it, when the objects for which it was commenced have been obtained; when once fairly entered, you will be borne along by the irresistable force of pride, habit of command, and, indeed, for self-preservation, and it will be impossible to recede.

But, it is said, that it is for the benefit of the People that the proposed change is to be made; and that by your talents and influence, alone, aided by unlimited power, the ambitious chiefs in the different departments are to be restrained, and the integrity of the republic preserved. I have said, and I most sincerely believe, that, from the state into which the country has been brought, that you alone can preserve it from the horrors of anarchy. But I cannot conceive that any extraordinary powers are necessary. The authority to see that the laws are executed; to call out the strength of the country, to enforce their execution, is all that is required, and is what is possessed by the Chief Magistrate of the United States, and of every other Republic; and is what was confided to the Executive, by the Constitution of Cucuta. Would your talents or your energies be impaired in the council, or the field, or your influence lessened, when acting as the head of a Republic?

I propose to examine, very briefly, the results which are likely to flow from the proposed change of government.... Depend on it, sir, that the moment which shall announce the continuance of arbitrary power in your hands, will be the commencement of commotions which will require all your talents and energies to supress. You may succeed. The disciplined army, at your disposal, may be too powerful for an unarmed, undisciplined, and scattered population; but one unsuccessful effort will not content them, and your feelings will be eternally racked by being obliged to make war upon those who have been accustomed to call you their father, and to invoke blessings on your head, and for no cause but their adherence to principles which you yourself had taught them to regard more than their lives.

If by the strong government which the advocates for the proposed change so strenuously recommend, one without responsibility is intended, which may put men to death, and immure them in dungeons, without trial, and one where the army is every thing, and the people nothing, I must say, that, if the tranquillity of Colombia is to be preserved in this way, the wildest anarchy would be preferable. Out of that anarchy a better government might arise; but the chains of military despotism once fastened upon a nation, ages might pass away before they could be shaken off.

But I contend that the strongest of all governments is that which is most free. We consider that of the United States as the strongest, precisely, because it is the most free. It possesses the faculties, equally to protect itself from foreign force or internal convulsion. In both, it has been sufficiently tried. In no country upon earth, would an armed opposition to the laws be sooner or more effectually put down. Not so much by the terrors of the guillotine and the gibbet, as from the aroused determination of the nation, exhibiting their strength, and convincing the factious that their cause was hopeless. No, sir, depend upon it, that the possession of arbitrary power, by the government of Colombia, will not be the means of securing its tranquillity; nor will the danger of disturbances solely arise from the opposition of the people. The power, and the military force which it will be necessary to put in the hands of the Governors of the distant provinces, added to the nature of the country, will continually present to those officers the temptation, and the means of revolt.

* * * *

From a knowledge of your own disposition, and present feelings, your Excellency will not be willing to believe, that you could ever be brought to commit an act of tyranny, or even to execute justice with unnecessary rigor. But trust me, sir, that there is nothing more corrupting, nothing more destructive of the noblest and finest feelings of our nature, than the exercise of unlimited power. The man who, in the beginning of such a career, might shudder at the idea of taking away the life of a fellow-being, might soon have his conscience so scared by the repetition of crime, that the agonies of his murdered victims might become music to his soul, and the drippings of his scaffold afford "blood enough to swim in." History is full of such examples.

From this disgusting picture, permit me to call the attention of your Excellency to one of a different character. It exhibits you as the constitutional Chief Magistrate of a free people. Giving to their representatives the influence of your great name and talents, to reform the abuses which, in a long reign of tyranny and misrule, have fastened upon every branch of the administration. The army, and its swarm of officers, reduced within the limits of real usefulness, placed on the frontiers, and no longer permitted to control public opinion, and be the terror of the peaceful citizen. By the removal of this incubus from the treasury, and the establishment of order, responsibility, and economy, in the expenditures of the Government, it would soon be enabled to dispense with the odious monopolies, and the duty of the <u>Alcavala</u>, which have operated with so malign an effect upon commerce and agriculture, and, indeed, upon the revenues which they were intended to augment. No longer oppressed by these shackles, industry would every where revive: the farmer and the artizan, cheered by the prospect of ample reward for their labor, would redouble their exertions; foreigners, with their capital and their skill in the arts, would crowd hither, to enjoy the advantages which could scarcely, elsewhere, be found....

* * * *

To yourself, the advantage would be as great as to the country; like acts of mercy, the blessings would be reciprocal; your personal happiness secured, and your fame elevated to a height which would leave but a single competition in the estimation of posterity. In bestowing the palm of merit, the world has become wiser than formerly. The successful warrior is no longer regarded as entitled to the first place in the temple of fame. Talents of this kind have become too common, and too often used for mischievous purposes to be regarded as they once were. In this enlightened age, the mere hero of the field, and the successful leader of armies, may, for the moment, attract attention. But it will be such as is bestowed upon the passing meteor, whose blaze is no longer remembered, when it is no longer seen. To be esteemed eminently great, it is necessary to be eminently good. The qualities of the Hero and the General must be devoted to the advantage of mankind, before he will be permitted to assume the title of their benefactor; and the station which he will hold in their regard and affections will depend, not upon the number and the splendor of his victories, but upon the results and the use he may make of the influence he acquires from them.

* * * *

To the eyes of military men, the laurels you won on the fields of Vargas, Bayaca, and Carrebobo, will be forever green; but will that content you? Are you willing that your name should descend to posterity, amongst the mass of those whose fame has been derived from shedding human blood, without a single advantage to the human race? Or, shall it be united to that of Washington, as the founder and the father of a great and happy people? The choice is before you. The friends of liberty throughout the world, and the people of the United States, in particular, are waiting your decision with intense anxiety. Alexander toiled and conquered to attain the applause of the Athenians; will you regard as nothing the opinions of a nation which has evinced its superiority over that celebrated people, in the science most useful to man, by having carried into actual practice a system of government, of which the wisest Athenians had but a glimpse in theory, and considered as a blessing never to be realised, however ardently to be desired? The place which you are to occupy in their esteem depends upon yourself. Farewell.

W. H. HARRISON

LETTER TO NILE'S WEEKLY REGISTER

North Bend, Ohio, May 1, 1836

*The Whig presidential campaign of 1840 was based on the
log cabin and hard cider theme and the military reputation
of its candidate. Little was said on the issues with the
exception that the voters would cast their ballots against
the policies of Van Buren, associated with the Panic of
1837. Harrison said very little, maintaining that his positions on the vital issues of the day had already been
made clear in letters such ·as the one below sent in response to a series of questions submitted by Sherrod
Williams of Niles' Weekly Register in 1836.*

North Bend, May 1, 1836

SIR: I have the honor to acknowledge the receipt of your letter of the
7th ultimo, in which you request me to answer the following questions:

1st. "Will you, if elected president of the United States, sign and
approve a bill distributing the surplus revenue of the United States
to each state, according to the federal population of each, for internal
improvement, education, and to such other objects as the legislatures
of the several states may see fit to apply the same?"

2d. "Will you sign and approve a bill distributing the proceeds of
the sales of the public lands to each state according to the federal
population of each, for the purposes above specified?"

3d. "Will you sign and approve bills making appropriations to improve navigable streams above ports of entry?"

4th. "Will you sign and approve (if it becomes necessary to secure
and save from depreciation the revenue and finances of the nation, and
to afford a uniform sound currency to the people of the United States)
a bill, (with proper modifications and restrictions) chartering a bank
of the United States?"

5th. "What is your opinion as to the constitutional power of the
senate or house of representatives of the congress of the United States,
to expunge or obliterate from the journals the records and proceedings
of a previous session?"

From the manner in which the four first questions are stated, it
appears that you do not ask my opinion as to the policy or propriety
of the measures to which they respectively refer; but what would be
my course, if they were presented to me (being in the presidential
chair of the United States) in the shape of bills, that had been duly
passed by the senate and house of representatives.

From the opinions which I have formed of the intention of the constitution, as to the cases in which the veto power should be exercised by the president, I would have contented myself with giving an affirmative answer to the four first questions, but, from the deep interest which has been, and indeed is now, felt in relation to all these subjects, I think it proper to express my views upon each one separately.

I answer, then, 1st. That the immediate return of all the surplus money which is or ought to be in the treasury of the United States, to the possession of the people, from whom it was taken, is called for by every principle of policy and indeed of safety to our institutions and I know of no mode of doing it better than that recommended by the present chief magistrate, in his first annual message to congress, in the following words: "To avoid these evils, it appears to me that the most safe, just and federal disposition which could be made of the surplus revenue, would be its apportionment among the several states, according to the ratio of representation."

This proposition has reference to a state of things which now actually exists, with the exception of the amount of money thus to be disposed of- for it could not have been anticipated by the president that the surplus above the real wants or convenient expenditures of the government would become so large, as that retaining it in the treasury would so much diminish the circulating medium as greatly to embarass the business of the country.

What other disposition can be made of it with a view to get it into immediate circulation, but to place it in the hands of the state authorities? So great is the amount, and so rapidly is it increasing, that it could not be expended for a very considerable time on the comparatively few objects to which it could be appropriated by the general government; but the desired distribution amongst the people could be immediately effected by the states from the infinite variety of ways in which it might be employed by them. By them it might be loaned to their own banking institutions, or even to individuals — a mode of distribution by the general government which, I sincerely hope, is in the contemplation of no friend to his country.

2d. Whilst, I have always broadly admitted that the public lands were the common property of all the states, I have been the advocate of that mode of disposing of them which would create the greatest number of freeholders, and I conceived that in this way the interest of all would be as well secured as by any other disposition; but since, by the small size of the tracts in which the lands are laid out, and the reduction of the price, this desirable situation is easily attainable by any person of tolerable industry, I am perfectly reconciled to the distribution of the proceeds of the sales as provided for by the bill introduced into the senate by Mr. Clay; the interest of all seems to be well provided for by this bill; and as from the opposition which has hitherto been made to the disposition of the lands hertofore contemplated by the representatives of the new states, there is no probability of its being adopted, I think it ought no longer to be insisted on.

3d. As I believe that no money should be taken from the treasury of the United States to be expended on internal improvements but for those which are strictly national, the answer to this question would be easy but from the difficulty of determining which of those that are from time to time proposed would be of this description. This circumstance, the excitement which has already been produced by appropriations of this kind, and the jealousies which it will no doubt continue to produce if persisted in, give additional claims to the mode of appropriating all the surplus revenue of the United States in the manner above suggested. Each state will then have the means of accomplishing its own schemes of internal improvement. Still there will be particular cases when a contemplated improvement will be of greater advantage to the union generally, and some particular states, than to that in which it is to be made. In such cases, as well as those in the new states, where the value of the public domain will be greatly enhanced by an improvement in the means of communication, the general government should certainly largely contribute. To appropriations of the latter character there has never been any very warm opposition. Upon the whole, the distribution of the surplus revenue amongst the states seems likely to remove most if not all, the causes of dissention of which the internal improvement system has been the fruitful source. There is nothing, in my opinion, more sacredly incumbent upon those who are concerned in the administration of our government than that of preserving harmony between the states. From the construction of our system there has been, and probably ever will be, more or less jealousy between the general and state governments; but there is nothing in the constitution-nothing in the character of the relation which the states bear to each other-which can create any unfriendly feeling, if the common guardian administers its favors with an even and impartial hand. That this may be the case, all those to whom any portion of this delicate power is entrusted should always act upon the principles of forbearance and conciliation; ever more ready to sacrifice the interest of their immediate constituents rather than violate the rights of the other members of the family. Those who pursue a different course, whose rule is never to stop short of the attainment of all which they may consider their due, will often be found to have trespassed upon the boundary they had themselves established.

*   *   *   *

4th. I have before me a newspaper, in which I am designated by its distinguished editor ''the bank and federal candidate.'' I think it would puzzle the writer to adduce any act of my life which warrants him in identifying me with the interest of the first, or the politics of the latter. Having no means of ascertaining the sentiments of the directors and stockholders of the bank of the United States (which is the one, I presume, with which it was intended to associate me) I cannot say what their course is likely to be in relation to the ensuing election for president. Should they, however, give me their support, it will be evidence at least that the opposition which I gave to their institution in my capacity of representative from Ohio in congress proceeded, in their opinion, from a sense of duty which I could not disregard.

The journals of the second session of the thirteenth, and those of the fourteenth congress, will show that my votes are recorded against them upon every question in which their interests was involved. I did, indeed, exert myself in the senate of Ohio to procure a repeal of the law which had imposed an enormous tax upon the branches which had been located in its boundaries at the request of the citizens. The ground of those exertions was not the interest of the bank; but to save what I considered the honor of the state, and to prevent a controversy between the state officers and those of the United States.

In the spring of 1834, I had also the honor to preside at a meeting of the citizens of Hamilton county called for the purpose of expressing their sentiments in relation to the removal of the public money from the custody of the bank by the sole authority of the executive. As president of the meeting, I explained at some length the object for which it was convened; but I advanced no opinion in relation to the recharter of the bank.

A most respectful memorial to the president in relation to the removal of the deposits was adopted, as were also resolutions in favor of rechartering the bank; but, as I have already said, this was not the purpose for which the meeting was called, and not one upon which, as presiding officer, I was called upon to give an opinion, but in the event of an equal division of the votes.

As a private citizen, no man can be more entirely clear of any motive, either for the rechartering the old institution, or creating a new one, under the authority of the United States. I never had a single share in the former, nor indeed in any bank, with one exception; and that many years ago failed, with the loss of the entire stock. I have no inclination again to venture in that way, even if I should ever possess the means. With the exception above mentioned, of stock in a bank long since broken, I never put out a dollar at interest in my life. My interest being entirely identified with the cultivation of the soil, I am immediately and personally connected with none other.

I have made this statement to show you that I am not commited to any course in relation to the chartering of a bank of the United States; and that I might, if so disposed, join in the popular cry of denunciation against the old institution, and upon its misconduct predicate an opposition to the chartering of another.

I shall not, however, take this course so opposite to that which I hope I have followed through life, but will give you my sentiments clearly and fully, not only with regard to the future conduct of the government on the subject of a national bank, but in relation to the operations of that which is now defunct.

I was not in congress when the late bank was chartered, but was a member of the thirteenth congress, after its first session, when the conduct of the bank in its incipient measures, was examined into; and believing from the result of the investigation that the charter had been violated, I voted for the judicial investigation; with a view of annuling its charter. The resolution for that purpose, however, failed; and shortly after, the management of its affairs was committed to the talents and integrity of Mr. Cheves. From that period to its final dissolution, (although I must confess I am not a very competent judge of such matters), I have no idea that an institution could have been conducted with more ability, integrity and public advantage, than it has been.

Under these impressions, I agree with gen. Jackson in the opinion expressed in one of his messages to congress, from which I make the following extract: "that a bank of the United States, competent to all the duties which may be required by the government, might be so organized as not to infringe on our delegated powers, or the reserved rights of the states, I do not entertain a doubt."* But the period for rechartering the old institution has passed, as Pennsylvania has wisely taken care to appropriate to herself the benefits of its large capital. The question then, for me to answer, is, whether, under the circumstances you state, if elected to the office of president, I would, sign an act to charter another bank, to answer, I would, if it were clearly ascertained that the public interest, in relation to the collection and disbursement of the revenue would materially suffer without one, and there were unequivocal manifestations of public opinion in its favor. I think, however, the experiment should be fairly tried, to ascertain whether the financial operations of the government cannot be as well carried on without the aid of a national bank. If it is not necessary for that purpose, it does not appear to me that one can be constitutionally chartered. There is no construction which I can give the constitution which would authorise it, on the ground of affording facilities to commerce. The measure, if adopted, must have for its object the carrying into effect (facilitating at least the exercise of) some of the powers positively granted to the general government. If others flow from it, producing equal advantages to the nation, so

---

* Niles' Register, vol 42, page 368.

much the better; but these cannot be made the ground for justifying a recourse to it.

The excitement which has been produced by the bank question, the number and respectability of those who deny the right to congress to charter one, strongly recommend the course above suggested.

5th. I distinctly answer to this question, that, in my opinion, neither house of congress can constitutionally expunge the record of the proceedings of their predecessors. The power to rescind certainly belongs to them; and is, for every public legitimate purpose, all that is necessary. The attempt to expunge a part of their journal, now making in the senate of the United States, I am satisfied could never have been made but in a period of the highest party excitement, when the voice of reason and generous feeling is stifled by long protracted and bitter controversy.

* * * *

INAUGURAL ADDRESS
March 4, 1841

No other inaugural address has been ridiculed in the way that Harrison's has. Seager, in his biography on the General's running mate and successor, And Tyler Too, *asserts that it was the worst ever delivered. It was certainly unduly long for the occasion of an inauguration, but it is possible that its reputation owes more to the colorful Roman proconsul-slaying criticism reportedly made by Webster the night before than to careful reading of the address itself.*

Harrison gained the presidency after the administrations of Jackson and Van Buren during which he saw the executive become much more powerful than he considered safe. He had also seen the dangers of excessive power in Colombia. The address, therefore, emphasizes what he would refrain from doing as President rather than what he would do. Most notable was his declaration that he would not run for reelection in 1844.

INAUGURAL ADDRESS

Called from a retirement which I had supposed was to continue for the residue of my life to fill the chief executive office of this great and free nation, I appear before you, fellow-citizens, to take the oaths which the Constitution prescribes as a necessary qualification for the performance of its duties; and in obedience to a custom coeval with our Government and what I believe to be your expectations I proceed to present to you a summary of the principles which will govern me in the discharge of the duties which I shall be called upon to perform.

It was the remark of a Roman consul in an early period of that celebrated Republic that a most striking contrast was observable in the conduct of candidates for offices of power and trust before and after obtaining them, they seldom carrying out in the latter case the pledges and promises made in the former. However much the world may have improved in many respects in the lapse of upward of two thousand years since the remark was made by the virtuous and indignant Roman, I fear that a strict examination of the annals of some of the modern elective governments would develop similar instances of violated confidence.

Although the fiat of the people has gone forth proclaiming me the Chief Magistrate of this glorious Union, nothing upon their part remaining to be done, it may be thought that a motive may exist to keep up the delusion under which they may be supposed to have acted in relation to my principles and opinions; and perhaps there may be some in this assembly who have come here either prepared to condemn those I shall now deliver, or, approving them, to doubt the sincerity with which they are now uttered. But the lapse of a few months will confirm or dispel their fears. The outline of principles to govern and measures to be adopted by an Administration not yet begun will soon be exchanged for immutable history, and I shall stand either exonerated by my countrymen or classed with the mass of those who promised that they might deceive and flattered with the intention to betray. However strong may by my present purpose to realize the expectations of a magnanimous and confiding people, I too well understand the dangerous temptations to which I shall be exposed from the magnitude of the power which it has been the pleasure of the people to commit to my hands not to place my chief confidence upon the aid of that Almighty Power which has hitherto protected me and enabled me to bring to favorable issues other important but still greatly inferior trusts heretofore confided to me by my country.

The broad foundation upon which our Constitution rests being the people- a breath of theirs having made, as a breath can unmake, change, or modify it — it can be assigned to none of the great divisions of government but that of democracy. If such is its theory, those who are called upon to administer it must recognize as its leading principle the duty of shaping their measure so as to produce the greatest good to the greatest number. But with these broad admissions, if we would compare the sovereignty acknowledged to exist in the mass of our people with the power claimed by other sovereignties, even by those which have been considered most purely democratic, we shall find a most essential difference. All others lay claim to power limited only by their own will. The majority of our citizens, on the contrary, possess a sovereignty with an amount of power precisely equal to that which has been granted to them by the parties to the national compact, and nothing beyond. We admit of no government by divine right, believing that so far as power is concerned the Beneficent Creator has made no distinction amongst men; that all are upon an equality, and that the only legitimate right to govern is an express grant of power from the governed. The Constitution of the United States is the instrument containing this grant of power to the several departments composing the Government. On an examination of that instrument it will be found to contain declarations of power granted and of power withheld. The latter is also susceptible of division into power which the majority had the right to grant, but which they did not think proper to intrust to their agents, and that which they could not have granted, not being possessed by themselves. In other words, there are certain rights possessed by each individual American citizen which in his compact with the others he has never surrendered. Some of them, indeed, he is unable to surrender, being, in the language of our system, unalienable. The boasted privilege of a Roman citizen was to him a shield only against a petty provincial ruler, whilst the proud democrat of Athens would console himself under a sentence of death for a supposed violation of the national faith — which no one understood and which at times was the subject of the mockery of all-or the banishment from his home, his family, and his country with or without an alleged cause, that it was the act not of a single tyrant or hated aristocracy, but of his assembled countrymen. Far different is the power of our sovereignty. It can interfere with no one's faith, prescribe forms of worship for no one's observance, inflict no punishment but after well-ascertained guilt, the result of investigation under rules prescribed by the Constitution itself. These precious privileges, and those scarcely less important of giving expression to his thoughts and opinions, either by writing or speaking, unrestrained but by the liability for injury to others, and that of a full participation in all the advantages which flow from the Government, the acknowledged property of all, the American citizen derives from no charter granted by his fellow-man. He claims them because he is himself a man, fashioned by the same Almighty hand as the rest of his species and entitled to a full share of the blessings with which He has endowed them. Notwithstanding the limited sovereignty possessed by the people of the United States and the restricted grant of power to the Government which they have adopted, enough has been given to accomplish all the objects for which it was created. It has been found powerful in war, and hitherto justice has been administered, an intimate union effected, domestic tranquility preserved, and personal liberty secured to the citizen. As was to be expected, however, from the defect of language and the necessarily sententious manner in which the Constitution is written, disputes have arisen as to the amount of power which it has actually granted or was intended to grant.

This is more particularly the case in relation to that part of the instrument which treats of the legislative branch, and not only as regards the exercise of powers claimed under a general clause giving that body the authority to pass all laws necessary to carry into effect the specified powers, but in relation to the latter also. It is, however, consolatory to reflect that most of the instances of alleged departure from the letter or spirit of the Constitution have ultimately received the sanction of a majority of the people. And the fact that many of our statesmen most distinguished for talent and patriotism have been at one time or other of their political career on both sides of each of the most warmly disputed questions forces upon us the inference that the errors, if errors there were, are attributable to the intrinsic difficulty in many instances of ascertaining the intentions of the framers of the Constiution rather than the influence of any sinister or unpatriotic motive. But the great danger to our institutions does not appear to me to be in a usurpation by the Government of power not granted by the people, but by the accumulation in one of the departments of that which was assigned to others. Limited as are the powers which have been granted, still enough have been granted to constitute a despotism if concentrated in one of the departments. This danger is greatly heightened, as it has been always observable that men are less jealous of encroachments of one department upon another than upon their own reserved rights. When the Constitution of the United States first came from the hands of the Convention which formed it, many of the sternest republicans of the day were alarmed at the extent of the power which had been granted to the Federal Government, and more particularly of that portion which had been assigned to the executive branch. There were in it features which appeared not to be in harmony with their ideas of a simple representative democracy or republic, and knowing the tendency of power to increase itself, particularly when exercised by a single individual, predictions were made that at no very remote period the Government would terminate in virtual monarchy. It would not become me to say that the fears of these patriots have been already realized; but as I sincerely believe that the tendency of measures and of men's opinions for some years past has been in that direction, it is, I conceive, strictly proper that I should take this occasion to repeat the assurances I have heretofore given of my determination to arrest the progress of that tendency if it really exists and restore the Government to its pristine health and vigor, as far as this can be effected by any legitimate exercise of the power placed in my hands.

I proceed to state in as summary a manner as I can my opinion of the sources of the evils which have been so extensively complained of and the correctives which may be applied. Some of the former are unquestionably to be found in the defects of the Constitution; others, in my judgment, are attributable to a misconstruction of some of its provisions. Of the former is the eligibility of the same individual to a second term of the Presidency. The sagacious mind of Mr. Jefferson early saw and lamented this error, and attempts have been made, hitherto without success, to apply the amendatory power of the States to its correction. As, however, one mode of correction is in the power of every President and consequently in mine, it would be useless, and perhaps invidious, to enumerate the evils of which, in the opinion of many of our fellow-citizens, this error of the sages who framed the Constitution may have been the source and the bitter fruits which we are still to gather from it if it continues to disfigure our system. It may be observed, however, as a general remark, that republics can commit no greater error than to adopt or continue any feature in their systems of government which may be calculated to create or increase the love of power in the bosoms of those to whom necessity obliges them to commit the management of their affairs; and surely nothing is more likely to produce such a state of mind than the long continuance of an office of high trust. Nothing can be more corrupting, nothing more destructive of all those noble feelings which belong to the character of a devoted republican patriot. When this corrupting passion once takes possession of the human mind, like the love of gold it becomes insatiable. It is the never-dying worm in his bosom, grows with his growth and strengthens with the declining years of its victim. If this is true, it is the part of wisdom for a republic to limit the service of that officer at least to whom she has intrusted the management of her foreign relations, the execution of her laws, and the command of her armies and navies to a period so short as to prevent his forgetting that he is the accountable agent, not the principal; the servant, not the master. Until an amendment of the Constitution can be effected public opinion may secure the desired object. I give my aid to it by renewing the pledge heretofore given that under no circumstances will I consent to serve a second term.

But if there is danger to public liberty from the acknowledged defects of the Constitution in the want of limit to the continuance of the Executive power in the same hands, there is, I apprehend, not much less from a misconstruction of that instrument as it regards the powers actually given. I can not conceive that by a fair construction any or either of its provisions would be found to constitute the President a part of the legislative power. It can not be claimed from the power to recommend, since, although enjoined as a duty upon him, it is a privilege which he holds in common with every other citizen; and although there may be something more of confidence in the propriety of the measures recommended in the one case than in the other, in the obligations of ultimate decision there can be no difference. In the language of the Constitution, "all the legislative powers" which it grants "are vested in the Congress of the United States." It would be a solecism in language to say that any portion of these is not included in the whole.

It may be said, indeed, that the Constitution has given to the Executive the power to annul the acts of the legislative body by refusing to them his assent. So a similar power has necessarily resulted from that instrument to the judiciary, and yet the judiciary forms no part of the Legislature. There is, it is true, this difference between these grants of power: The Executive can put his negative upon the acts of the Legislature for other cause than that of want of conformity to the Constitution, whilst the judiciary can only declare void those which violate that instrument. But the decision of the judiciary is final in such a case, whereas in every instance where the veto of the Executive is applied it may be overcome by a vote of two-thirds of both Houses of Congress. The negative upon the acts of the legislative by the executive authority, and that in the hands of one individual, would seem to be an incongruity in our system. Like some other of a similar character, however, it appears to be highly expedient, and if used only with the forebearance and in the spirit which was intended by its authors it may be productive of great good and be found one of the best safeguards to the Union. At the period of the formation of the Constitution the principle does not appear to have enjoyed much favor in the State governments. It existed but in two, and in one of these there was a plural executive. If we would search for the motives which operated upon the purely patriotic and enlightened assembly which framed the Constitution for the adoption of a provision so apparently repugnant to the leading democratic principle that the majority should govern, we must reject the idea that they anticipated from it any benefit to the ordinary course of legislation. They knew too well the high degree of intelligence which existed among the people and the enlightened character of the State Legislatures not to have the fullest confidence that the two bodies elected by them would be worthy representatives of such constituents, and, of course, that they would require no aid in conceiving and maturing the measures which the circumstances of the country might require. And it is preposterous to suppose that a thought could for a moment have been entertained that the President, placed at the capital, in the center of the country, could better understand the wants and wishes of the people than their own immediate representatives, who spend a part of every year among them living with them, often laboring with them, and bound to them by the triple tie of interest, duty, and affection. To assist or control Congress, then, in its ordinary legislation could not, I conceive, have been the motive for conferring the veto power on the President. This argument acquires additional force from the fact of its never having been thus used by the first six Presidents–and two of them were members of the Convention, one presiding over its deliberations and the other bearing a larger share in consummating the labors of that august body than any other person. But if bills were never returned to Congress by either of the Presidents above referred to upon the ground of their being inexpedient or not as well adapted as they might be to the wants of the people, the veto was applied upon that of want of conformity to the Constitution or because errors had been committed from a too hasty enactment.

There is another ground for the adoption of the veto principle, which had probably more influence in recommending it to the Convention than any other. I refer to the security which it gives to the just and equitable action of the Legislature upon all parts of the Union. It could not but have occurred to the Convention that in a country so extensive, embracing so great a variety of soil and climate, and consequently of products, and which from the same causes must ever exhibit a great difference in the amount of the population of its various sections, calling for a great diversity in the employments of the people, that the legislation of the majority might not always justly regard the rights and interests of the minority, and that acts of this character might be passed under an express grant by the words of the Constitution, and therefore not within the competency of the judiciary to declare void; that however enlightened and patiotic they might suppose from past experience the members of Congress might be, and however largely partaking, in the general, of the liberal feelings of the people, it was impossible to expect that bodies so constituted should not sometimes be controlled by local interests and sectional feelings. It was proper, therefore, to provide some umpire from whose situation and mode of appointment more independence and freedom from such influences might be expected. Such a one was afforded by the executive department constiuted by the Constitution. A person elected to that high office, having his constituents in every section, State, and subdivision of the Union, must consider himself bound by the most solemn sanctions to guard, protect, and defend the rights of all and of every portion, great or small, from the injustice and oppression of the rest. I consider the veto power, therefore, given by the Constitution to the Executive of the United States solely as a conservative power, to be used only, first, to protect the Constitution from violation; secondly, the people from the effects of hasty legislation where their will has been probably disregarded or not well understood, and, thirdly, to prevent the effects of combinations violative of the rights of minorities. In reference to the second of these objects I may observe that I consider it the right and privilege of the people to decide disputed points of the Constitution arising from the general grant of power to Congress to carry into effect the powers expressly given; and I believe with Mr. Madison that "repeated recognitions under varied circumstances in acts of the legislative, executive, and judicial branches of the Government, accompanied by indications in different modes of the concurrence of the general will of the nation," as affording to the President sufficient authority for his considering such disputed points as settled.

Upward of half a century has elapsed since the adoption of the present form of government. It would be an object more highly desirable than the gratification of the curiosity of speculative statesmen if its precise situation could be ascertained, a fair exhibit made of the operations of each of its departments, of the powers which they respectively claim and exercise, of the collisions which have occurred between them or between the whole Government and those of the States or either of them. We could then compare our actual condition after fifty years' trial of our system with what it was in the commencement of its operations and ascertain whether the predictions of the patriots who opposed its adoption or the confident hopes of its advocates have been best realized. The great dread of the former seems to have been that the reserved powers of the States would be absorbed by those of the Federal Government and a consolidated power established, leaving to the States the shadow only of that independent action for which they had so zealously contended and on the preservation of which they relied as the last hope of liberty. Without denying that the result to which they looked with so much apprehension is in the way of being realized, it is obvious that they did not clearly see the mode of its accomplishment. The General Government has seized upon none of the

Reserved rights of the States. As far as any open warfare may have gone, the State authorities have amply maintained their rights. To a casual observer our system presents no appearance of discord between the different members which compose it. Even the addition of many new ones has produced no jarring. They move in their respective orbits in perfect harmony with the central head and with each other. But there is still an undercurrent at work by which, if not seasonably checked, the worst apprehensions of our anti-federal patriots will be realized, and not only will the State authorities be overshadowed by the great increase of power in the executive department of the General Government, but the character of that Government, if not its designation, be essentially and radically changed. This state of things has been in part effected by causes inherent in the Constitution and in part by the never-failing tendency of political power to increase itself. By making the President the sole distributer of all the patronage of the Government the framers of the Constitution do not appear to have anticipated at how short a period it would become a formidable instrument to control the free operations of the State governments. Of trifling importance at first, it had early in Mr. Jefferson's Administration become so powerful as to create great alarm in the mind of that patriot from the potent influence it might exert in controlling the freedom of the elective franchise. If such could have then been the effects of its influence, how much greater must be the danger at this time, quadrupled in amount as it certainly is and more completely under the control of the Executive will than their construction of their powers allowed or the forbearing characters of all the early Presidents permitted them to make. But it is not by the extent of its patronage alone that the executive department has become dangerous, but by the use which it appears may be made of the appointing power to bring under its control the whole revenues of the country. The Constitution has declared it to be the duty of the President to see that the laws are executed, and it makes him the Commander in Chief of the Armies and Navy of the United States. If the opinion of the most approved writers upon that species of mixed government which in modern Europe is termed monarchy in contradistinction to despotism is correct, there was wanting no other addition to the powers of our Chief Magistrate to stamp a monarchical character on our Government but the control of the public finances; and to me it appears strange indeed that anyone should doubt that the entire control which the President possesses over the officers who have the custody of the public money, by the power of removal with or without cause, does, for all mischievous purposes at least, virtually subject the treasure also to his disposal. The first Roman Emperor, in his attempt to seize the sacred treasure, silenced the opposition of the officer to whose charge it had been committed by a significant allusion to his sword. By a selection of political instruments for the care of the public money a reference to their commissions by a President would be quite as effectual an argument as that of Caesar to the Roman knight. I am not insensible of the great difficulty that exists in drawing a proper plan for the safe-keeping and disbursement of the public revenues, and I know the importance which has been attached by men of great abilities and patriotism to the divorce, as it is called, of the Treasury from the banking institutions. It is not the divorce which is complained of, but the unhallowed union of the Treasury with the executive department, which has created such extensive alarm. To this danger to our republican institutions and that created by the influence given to the Executive through the instumentality of the Federal officers I propose to apply all the remedies which may be at my command. It was certainly a great error in the framers of the Constitution not to have made the officer at the head of the Treasury Department entirely independent of the Executive. He should at least have been removable only upon the demand of the popular branch of the Legislature. I have determined never to remove a Secretary of the Treasury without communicating all the circumstances attending such removal to both Houses of Congress.

The influence of the Executive in controlling the freedom of the elective franchise through the medium of the public officers can be effectually checked by renewing the prohibition published by Mr. Jefferson forbidding their interference in election further than giving their own votes, and their own independence secured by an assurance of perfect immunity in exercising this sacred privilege of freemen under the dictates of their own unbiased judgments. Never with my consent shall an officer of the people, compensated for his services out of their pockets, become the pliant instrument of Executive will.

There is no part of the means placed in the hands of the Executive which might be used with greater effect for unhallowed purposes than the control of the public press. The maxim which our ancestors derived from the mother country that "the freedom of the press is the great bulwark of civil and religious liberty" is one of the most precious legacies which they have left us. We have learned, too, from our own as well as the experience of other countries, that golden shackles, by whomsoever or by whatever pretense imposed, are as fatal to it as the iron bonds of despotism. The presses in the necessary employment of the Government should never be used "to clear the guilty or to varnish crime" A decent and manly examination of the acts of the Government should be not only tolerated, but encouraged.

Upon another occasion I have given my opinion at some length upon the impropriety of Executive interference in the legislation of Congress — that the article in the Constiution making it the duty of the President to communicate information and authorizing him to reccomend measures was not intended to make him the source in legislation, and, in particular, that he should never be looked to for schemes of finance. It would be very strange, indeed, that the Constitution should have strictly forbidden one branch of the Legislature from interfering in the origination of such bills and that it should be considered proper that an altogether different department of the Government should be permitted to do so. Some of our best political maxims and opinions have been drawn from our parent isle. There are others, however, which can not be introduced in our system without singular incongruity and the production of much mischief, and this I conceive to be one. No matter in which of the houses of Parliament a bill may originate nor by whom introduced-a minister or a member of the opposition-by the fiction of law, or rather of constitutional principle, the sovereign is supposed to have prepared it agreeably to this will and then submitted it to Parliament for their advice and consent. Now the very reverse is the case here, not only with regard to the principle, but the forms prescribed by the Constitution. The principle certainly assigns to the only body constituted by the Constitution (the legislative body) the power to make laws, and the forms even direct that the enactment should be ascribed to them. The Senate, in relation to revenue bills, have the right to propose amendments, and so has the Executive by the power given him to return them to the House of Representatives with his objections. It is in his power also to propose amendments in the existing revenue laws, suggested by his observations upon their defective or injurious operation. But the delicate duty of devising schemes of revenue should be left where the Constitution has placed it-with the immediate representatives of the people. For similar reasons the mode of keeping the public treasure should be prescribed by them, and the further removed it may be from control of the Executive the more wholesome the arrangement and the more in accordance with republican principle.

Connected with this subject is the character of the currency. The idea of making it exclusively metallic, however well intended, appears to me to be fraught with more fatal consequences than any other scheme having no relation to the personal rights of the citizens that has ever been devised. If any single scheme could produce the effect of arresting at once that mutation of condition by which thousands of our most indigent fellow-citizens by their industry and enterprise are raised to the possession of wealth, that is the one. If there is one measure better calculated than another to produce that state of things so much deprecated by all true republicans, by which the rich are daily adding to their hoards and the poor sinking deeper into penjury, it is an exclusive metallic currency. Or if there is a process by which the character of the country for generosity and nobleness of feeling may be destroyed by the great increase and necessary toleration of usury, it is an exclusive metallic currency.

Amongst the other duties of a delicate character which the President is called upon to perform is the supervision of the government of the Territories of the United States. Those of them which are destined to become members of our great political family are compensated by their rapid progress from infancy to manhood for the partial and temporary deprivation of their political rights. It is in this District only where American citizens are to be found who under a settled policy are deprived of many important political privileges without any inspiring hope as to the future. Their only consolation under circumstances of such deprivation is that of the devoted exterior guards of a camp — that their sufferings secure tranquility and safety within. Are there any of their countrymen who would subject them to greater sacrifices to any other humiliations than those essentially necessary to the security of the object for which they were thus separated from their fellow-citizens? Are their rights alone not to be guaranteed by the application of those great principles upon which all our constitutions are founded? We are told by the greatest of British orators and statesmen that at the commencement of the War of the Revolution the most stupid men in England spoke of "their American subjects." Are there, indeed, citizens of any of our States who have dreamed of their subjects in the District of Columbia? Such dreams can never be realized by any agency of mine. The people of the District of Columbia are not the subjects of the people of the States, but free American citizens. Being in the latter condition when the Constitution was formed, no words used in that instrument could have been intended to deprive them of that character. If there is anything in the great principle of unalienable rights so emphatically insisted upon in our Declaration of Independence, they could neither make nor the United States accept a surrender of their liberties and become the subjects — in other words, the slaves — of their former fellow-citizens. If this be true — and it will scarcely be denied by anyone who has a correct idea of his own rights as an American citizen—the grant to Congress of exclusive jurisdiction in the District of Columbia can be interpreted, so far as respects the aggregate people of the United States, as meaning nothing more than to allow to Congress the controlling power necessary to afford a free and safe exercise of the functions assigned to the General Government by the Constitution. In all other respects the legislation of Congress should be adapted to their peculiar position and wants and be conformable with their deliberate opinions of their own interests.

I have spoken of the necessity of keeping the respective departments of the Government, as well as all the other authorities of our country, within their appropriate orbits. This is a matter of difficulty in some cases, as the powers which they respectively claim are often not defined by any distinct lines. Mischievous, however, in their tendencies as collisions of this kind may be, those which arise between the respective communities which for certain purposes compose one nation are much more so, for no such nation can long exist without the careful culture of those feelings of confidence and affection which are the effective bonds to union between free and confederated states. Strong as is the tie of interest, it has been often found ineffectual. Men blinded by their passions have been known to adopt measures for their country in direct opposition to all the suggestions of policy. The alternative, then, is to destroy or keep down a bad passion by creating and fostering a good one, and this seems to be the corner stone upon which our American political architects have reared the fabric of our Government. The cement which was to bind it and perpetuate its existence was the affectionate attachment between all its members. To insure the continuance of this feeling, produced at first by a community of dangers, of sufferings, and of interests, the advantages of each were made accessible to all. No participation in any good possessed by any member of our extensive Confederacy, except in domestic government, was withheld from the the citizen of any other member. By a process attended with no difficulty, no delay, no expense but that of removal, the citizen of one might become the citizen of any other, and successively of the whole. The lines, too, separating powers to be exercised by the citizens of one State from those of another seem to be so distinctly drawn as to leave no room for misunderstanding. The citizens of each State unite in their persons all the privileges which that character confers and all that they may claim as citizens of the United States, but in no case can the same persons at the same time act as the citizen of two separate States, and he is therefore positively precluded from any interference with the reserved powers of any State but that of which he is for the time being a citizen. He may, indeed, offer to the citizens of other States his advice as to their management, and the form in which it is tendered is left to his own discretion and sense of propriety. It may be observed, however, that organized associations of citizens requiring compliance with their wishes too much resemble the recommendations of Athens to her allies, supported by an armed and powerful fleet. It was, indeed, to the ambition of the leading States of Greece to control the domestic concerns of the others that the destruction of that celebrated Confederacy, and subsequently of all its members, is mainly to be attributed, and it is owing to the absence of that spirit that the Helvetic Confederacy has for so many years been preserved. Never has there been seen in the institutions of the separate members of any confederacy more elements of discord. In the principles and forms of government and religion, as well as in the circumstances of the several Cantons, so marked a discrepancy was observable as to promise anything but harmony in their intercourse or permanency in their alliance, and yet for ages neither has been interrupted. Content with the positive benefits which their union produced, with the independence and safety from foreign aggression which it secured, these sagacious people respected the institutions of each other, however repugnant to their own principles and prejudices.

Our Confederacy, fellow-citizens, can only be preserved by the same forbearance. Our citizens must be content with the exercise of the powers with which the Constitution clothes them. The attempt of those of one State to control the domestic institutions of another can only result in feelings of distrust and jealousy, the certain harbingers of disunion, violence, and civil war, and the ultimate destruction of our free institutions. Our Confederacy is perfectly illustrated by the terms and principles governing a common copartnership. There is a fund of power to be exercised under the direction of the joint councils of the allied members, but that which has been reserved by the individual members is intangible by the common Government or the individual members composing it. To attempt it finds no support in the principles of our Constitution.

It should be our constant and earnest endeavor mutually to cultivate a spirit of concord and harmony among the various parts of our Confederacy. Experience has abundantly taught us that the agitation by citizens of one part of the Union of a subject not confided to the General Government, but exclusively under the guardianship of the local authorities, is productive of no other consequences than bitterness, alienation, discord, and injury to the very cause which is intended to be advanced. Of all the great interest which appertain to our country, that of union – cordial, confiding, fraternal union – is by far the most important, since it is the only true and sure guaranty of all others.

In consequence of the embarrassed state of business and the currency, some of the States may meet with difficulty in their financial concerns. However deeply we may regret anything imprudent or excessive in the engagements into which States have entered for purposes of their own, it does not become us to disparage the State governments, nor to discourage them from making proper efforts for their own relief. On the contrary, it is our duty to encourage them to the extent of our constitutional authority to apply their best means and cheerfully to make all necessary sacrifices and submit to all necessary burdens to fulfill their engagements and maintain their credit, for the character and credit of the several States form a part of the character and credit of the whole country. The resources of the country are abundant, the enterprise and activity of our people proverbial, and we may well hope that wise legislation and prudent administration by the respective governments, each acting within its own sphere, will restore former prosperity.

Unpleasant and even dangerous as collisions may sometimes be between the constituted authorities of the citizens of our country in relation to the lines which separate their respective jurisdictions, the respective jurisdictions, the results can be of no vital injury to our institutions if that ardent patriotism, that devoted attachment to liberty, that spirit of moderation and forbearance for which our countrymen were once distinguished, continue to be cherished. If this continues to be the ruling passion of our souls, the weaker feeling of the mistaken enthusiast will be corrected, the Utopian dreams of the scheming politician dissipated, and the complicated intrigues of the demagogue rendered harmless. The spirit of liberty is the sovereign balm for every injury which our institutions may receive. On the contrary, no care that can be used in the construction of our Government, no division of powers, no distribution of checks in its several departments, will prove effectual to keep us a free people if this spirit is suffered to decay; and decay it will without constant nurture. To the neglect of this duty the best historians agree in attributing the ruin of all the republics with whose existence and fall their writings have made us acquainted. The same causes will ever produce the same effects, and as long as the love of power is a dominant passion of the human bosom, and as long as the understandings of men can be warped and their affections changed by operations upon their passions and prejudices, so long will the liberties of a people depend on their own constant attention to its preservation. The danger to all well-established free governments arises from the unwillingness of the people to believe in its existence or from the influence of designing men diverting their attention from the quarter whence it approaches to a source from which it can never come. This is the old trick of those who would usurp the government of their country. In the name of democracy they speak, warning the people against the influence of wealth and the danger of aristocracy. History, ancient and modern, is full of such examples. Caesar became the master of the Roman people and the senate under the pretense of supporting the democratic claims of the former against the aristocracy of the latter; Cromwell, in the character of protector of the liberties of the people, became the dictator of England, and Bolivar possessed himself of unlimited power with the title of his country's liberator. There is, on the contrary, no instance on record of an extensive and well-established republic being changed into an aristocracy. The tendencies of all such governments in their decline is to monarchy, and the antagonist principle to liberty there is the spirit of faction — a spirit which assumes the character and in times of great excitement imposes itself upon the people as the genuine spirit of freedom, and, like the false Christs whose coming was foretold by the Savior, seeks to, and were it possible would, impose upon the true and most faithful disciples of liberty. It is in periods like this that it behooves the people to be most watchful of those to whom they have intrusted power. And although there is at times much difficulty in distinguishing the false from the true spirit, a calm and dispassionate investigation will detect the counterfeit, as well by the character of its operations as the results that are produced. The true spirit of liberty, although devoted, persevering, bold, and uncompromising in principle, that secured is mild and tolerant and scrupulous as to the means it employs, whilst the spirit of party, assuming to be that of liberty, is harsh, vindictive, and intolerant, and totally reckless as to the character of the allies which it brings to the aid of its cause. When the genuine spirit of liberty animates the body of a people to a thorough examination of their affairs, it leads to the excision of every excrescence which may have fastened itself upon any of the departments of the government, and restores the system to its pristine health and beauty. But the reign of an intolerant spirit of party amongst a free people seldom fails to result in a dangerous accession to the executive power introduced and established amidst unusual professions of devotion to democracy.

The foregoing remarks relate almost exclusively to matters connected with our domestic concerns. It may be proper, however, that I should give some indications to my fellow-citizens of my proposed course of conduct in the management of our foreign relations. I assure them, therefore, that it is my intention to use every means in my power to preserve the friendly intercourse which now so happily subsists with every foreign nation, and that although, of course, not well informed as to the state of pending negotiations with any of them, I see in the personal characters of the sovereigns, as well as in the mutual interests of our own and of the governments with which our relations are most intimate, a pleasing guaranty that the harmony so important to the interests of their subjects as well as of our citizens will not be interrupted by the advancement of any claim or pretension upon their part to which our honor would not permit us to yield. Long the defender of my country's rights in the field, I trust that my fellow-citizens will not see in my earnest desire to preserve peace with foreign powers any indication that their rights will ever be sacrificed or the honor of the nation tarnished by any admission on the part of their Chief Magistrate unworthy of their former glory. In our intercourse with our aboriginal neighbors the same liberality and justice which marked the course prescribed to me by two of my illustrious predecessors when acting under their direction in the discharge of the duties of superintendent and commissioner shall be strictly observed. I can conceive of no more sublime spectacle, none more likely to propitiate an impartial and common Creator, than a rigid adherence to the principles of justice on the part of powerful nation in its transactions with a weaker and uncivilized people whom circumstances have placed at its disposal.

Before concluding, fellow-citizens, I must say something to you on the subject of the parties at this time existing in our country. To me it appears perfectly clear that the interest of that country requires that the violence of the spirit by which those parties are at this time governed must be greatly mitigated, if not entirely extinguished, or consequences will ensue which are appalling to be thought of.

If parties in a republic are necessary to secure a degree of vigilance sufficient to keep the public functionaries within the bounds of law and duty, at that point their usefulness ends. Beyond that they become destructive of public virtue, the parent of a spirit antagonist to that of liberty, and eventually its inevitable conqueror. We have examples of republics where the love of country and of liberty at one time were the dominant passions of the whole mass of citizens, and yet, with the continuance of the name and forms of free government, not a vestige of these qualities remaining in the bosoms of any one of its citizens. It was the beautiful remark of a distinguished English writer that "in the Roman senate Octavious had a party and Antony a party, but the Commonwealth had none." Yet the senate continued to meet in the temple of liberty to talk of the sacredness and beauty of the Commonwealth and gaze at the statues of the elder Brutus and of the Curtii and Decii, and the people assembled in the forum, not, as in the days of Camillus and the Scipios, to cast their free votes for annual magistrates or pass upon the acts of the senate, but to receive from the hands of the leaders of the respective parties their share of the spoils and to shout for one or the other, as those collected in Gaul or Egypt and the lesser Asia would furnish the larger dividend. The spirit of liberty had fled, and, avoiding the abodes of civilized man, had sought protection in the wilds of Scythia or Scandinavia; and so under the operation of the same causes and influences it will fly from our Capitol and our forums. A calamity so awful, not only to our country, but to the world, must be deprecated by every patriot and every tendency to a state of things likely to produce it immediately checked. Such a tendency has existed — does exist. Always the friend of my countrymen, never their flatterer, it becomes my duty to say to them from this high place to which their partiality has exalted me that there exists in the land a spirit hostile to their best interests — hostile to liberty itself. It is a spirit contracted in its views, selfish in its objects. It looks to the aggrandizement of a few even to the destruction of the interests of the whole. The entire remedy is with the people. Something, however, may be effected by the means which they have placed in my hands. It is union that we want, not of a party for the sake of that party, but a union of the whole country for the sake of the whole country, for the defense of its interests and its honor against foreign aggression, for the defense of those principles for which our ancestors so gloriously contended. As far as it depends upon me it shall be accomplished. All the influence that I possess shall be exerted to prevent the formation at least of an Executive party in the halls of the legislative body. I wish for the support of no member of that body to any measure of mine that does not satisfy his judgment and his sense of duty to those from whom he holds his appointment, nor any confidence in advance from the people but that asked for by Mr. Jefferson, "to give firmness and effect to the legal administration of their affairs."

I deem the present occasion sufficiently important and solemn to justify me in expressing to my fellow citizens a profound reverence for the Christian religion and a thorough conviction that sound morals, religious liberty, and a just sense of religious responsibility are essentially connected with all true and lasting happiness; and to that good Being who has blessed us by the gifts of civil and religious freedom, who watched over and prospered the labors of our fathers and has hitherto preserved to us institutions far exceeding in excellence those of any other people, let us unite in fervently commending every interest of our beloved country in all future time.

Fellow-citizens, being fully invested with that high office to which the partiality of my countrymen has called me, I now take an affectionate leave of you. You will bear with you to your homes the remembrance of the pledge I have this day given to discharge all the high duties of my exalted station according to the best of my ability, and I shall enter upon their performance with entire confidence in the support of a just and generous people.

March 4, 1841.

BIBLIOGRAPHICAL AIDS

The works cited below are some of the more important ones which shed light on William Henry Harrison and on the events and conditions which led to his elevation to the presidency. Since his actual stay in the White House was so brief, none of the works place much emphasis on it.

Because Harrison has not been a favorite subject of presidential biographers, it has not been necessary to be as selective in this bibliography as in many others in the series. An emphasis has, however, been placed on works that are recent and accessible. Additional titles may be found in Old Tippecanoe: William Henry Harrison and His Times (see Biographies below). A Bibliography of William Henry Harrison, John Tyler, James Polk, compiled by John W. Cronin and W. Harvey Wise, Riverford Publishing Co. (Washington, 1935), The Encyclopedia of American History, edited by Richard B. Morris, revised edition, Harper and Row (New York, 1965), the Harvard Guide to American History and the American Historical Association's Guide to Historical Literature. Additional essays can be found through Reader's Guide to Periodical Literature and the Social Science and Humanities Index.

An asterisk identifies a book that is currently available in paperback.

SOURCE MATERIALS

The largest collection of Harrison manuscript materials is in the Library of Congress. There are, however, few papers on the 1840 campaign or his brief presidency. Three reels of materials are available on microfilm in the Presidential Papers Microfilm series. Most of these are papers concerning his relations with the Indians, the War of 1812 and the campaign of 1836. Additional manuscript collections are in the Chicago Historical Society, the Indiana Historical Society, the New York Public Library, the Ohio State Library, the Cincinnati Historical Society and the private collection of John Scott Harrison IV.

Published sources of letters, reports and speeches of Harrison include:

American State Papers. Especially valuable are Volumes I and II of Indian Affairs which contain the instructions to Harrison, reports on his encounters and negotiations with the various tribes as Governor of the Indiana Territory, and the texts of the treaties signed.

Barnhart, John D. "Letters of William H. Harrison to Thomas Worthington, 1799-1813," Indiana Magazine of History, XLVII (March, 1951), 53-84. While many of these letters deal with personal and personal business matters they do contain many comments on issues. Light is shed on Harrison's ambitions.

Esary, Logan. Messages and Letters of William Henry Harrison. Volumes VII and IX of Governors' Messages and Letters, Indiana Historical Collections. Indianapolis, 1922.

Harrison, William Henry. Remarks of General William Henry Harrison, Late Envoy Extraordinary and Minister Plenipotentiary of the United States to the Republic of Colombia, on Certain Charges Made against Him by That Government to Which Is Added an Unofficial Letter, from General Harrison to General Bolivar, on the Affairs of Colombia; with Notes Explanatory of His Views of the Present State of that Country. Washington, 1830. The content is fully described in the title.

"Letter from William Henry Harrison to Harmar Denny of Pittsburgh, Accepting the Nomination to the Office of President of the United States, by the Convention of the Anti-Masonic Party, Held at Philadelphia, in the Fall of 1838," Western Pennsylvania Historical Magazine, I (July, 1918), 144-151. Contains a good brief statement of his concept of the presidency.

Richardson, James D. Messages and Papers of the Presidents, 1789-1897. Vol. IV. Washington, 1897.

BIOGRAPHIES

Cleaves, Freeman. Old Tippecanoe: William Henry Harrison and His Time. New York, 1939. The most recent and best available biography of Harrison. Based on extensive research, it provides balanced accounts of his military and political careers. It is well and interestingly written. While Harrison's faults are noted the overall picture of him is a favorable one. It contains an excellent bibliography. It will probably remain the standard work for some time.

Goebel, Dorothy Burne. William Henry Harrison; A Political Biography. Indianapolis, 1926. The first full biography since those written during his campaigns. The section concerning his attitude toward slavery is still the best available.

ESSAYS

There are several good articles on Harrison in the encyclopedias and collections. The best are those by Dorothy Burne Goebel in the Dictionary of American Biography, Stefan Lorant in the Encyclopedia Americana and George E. Mowry in Collier's Encyclopedia. Of the authors, the first is an authority on the man, the second on the presidency and the third on the times. Other essays on particular aspects of his life and career include:

Bond, Beverley Waugh, Jr. "William Henry Harrison in the War of 1812," Mississippi Valley Historical Review, XIII (March, 1967), 499-516. Generally favorable toward Harrison and highly critical of the national administration. Sees the victory at the Thames as a momentous one making Illinois and Indiana safe.

Booth, Edward Townsend. "William Henry Harrison: Ohio Alluvial," Country Life in America As Lived by Ten Presidents of the United States. New York, 1947, 148-168. Emphasizes the change in his life and career which resulted from his moving away from the decaying plantation at Berkeley Hundred to the frontier.

Dowdey, Clifford. "The Harrisons of Berkeley Hundred," American Heritage, VIII (April, 1957), 58-70.

Goebel, Dorothy Burne and Julius Goebel, Jr. "William Henry Harrison," Generals in the White House. Garden City, N.Y., 1945, 98-117. More critical of his military performance than Cleaves or Hitsman.

Marshall, Lynn L. "The Strange Stillbirth of the Whig Party," The American Historical Review, LXXII (January, 1967), 445-468.

Miles, Edwin A. "The Whig Party and the Menace of Caesar," Tennessee Historical Quarterly, XXVII (Winter, 1968), 361-379. Shows the influence of Roman history and fear of militarism that influenced the formation of the Whig Party and the difficulty resulting from the emergence of a military man, Harrison, as their candidate.

Peckham, Howard H. "Tears for Old Tippecanoe, Religious Inter-
pretations of President Harrison's Death," Proceedings of
the American Antiquarian Society, LXIX (April, 1959), 17-
36. Reactions to the first death of an American president
in office.

MONOGRAPHS AND SPECIAL AREAS

Bond, Beverley Waugh. The Civilization of the Old Northwest; A
Study of Political, Social and Economic Development 1788-
1812. New York, 1934. Harrison, as governor, is evaluated
in light of the context in which he operated.

Gunderson, Robert Gray. The Log-Cabin Campaign. Lexington, Ky.,
1957. Popularly written book on the campaign beginning with
the Panic of 1837.

Hitsman, J. Mackey. The Incredible War of 1812: A Military History.
Toronto, 1965. A Canadian military historian provides a generally favorable evaluation of Harrison's military performance.

Prucha, Francis Paul. American Indian Policy in the Formative
Years: The Indian Trade and Intercourse Acts 1790-1834.
Cambridge, Mass., 1962. Presents Harrison as one of the
individuals who had a genuine concern for the legal rights
of Indians but a zealous bargainer for land cessions in treaties.

NOTE ON MATERIALS ON THE PERIOD

With the exception of the War of 1812, the men and events related
to Harrison's presidency are the same as those related to Tyler's.
Two standard U.S. works on the War of 1812 are noted here and the
remainder of the works on the period are included among the Bibliographical Aids at the end of the section on Tyler.

Coles, Harry L. The War of 1812, [The Chicago History of American
Civilization,] Chicago, 1965.

Pratt, Julius W. Expansionists of 1812. Gloucester, Mass., 1957.

NOTE ON MATERIALS ON THE PRESIDENCY

Materials on the Presidency will be found in the Bibliographical Aids at the end of the section on Tyler.

JOHN TYLER
1790-1862

CHRONOLOGY

JOHN TYLER
TENTH PRESIDENT OF THE UNITED STATES

EARLY LIFE
AND POLITICAL CAREER

1790

March 29   Born at Greenway, an estate of 1,200 acres with 40 slaves, Charles City County, Virginia, the second of three sons in a family of eight children of Virginia Governor and United States Circuit Court Judge John Tyler and Mary Armistead Tyler.

1797

April   Mother, Mary Armistead Tyler, died at age 37.

1802

Entered the preparatory division (grammar school) of William and Mary

1807

July 4   Graduated from William and Mary. Delivered oration on the subject, "Female Education."

1811

Entered law practice in Charles City and was elected to the Virginia House of Delegates. Seated in December.

1812

January 14   Introduced resolution censuring United States Senators Brent and Giles of Virginia for not obeying the instructions of the House of Delegates to vote against renewal of the charter of the Bank of the United States. Resolution passed 97 to 20.

1813

January 6   Father, Judge John Tyler, died.

March 29   Married Letitia Christian of Cedar Grove planta-
                    tion, New Kent County, Virginia.

Summer   Joined local militia organized to defend Charles
                    City in the event of British attack. Commissioned
                    captain.

                              1815
April 15   Daughter, Mary, born.

                              1816
September 9   Son, Robert, born.

December 17   Entered United States House of Representative.

                              1818
November 30   Appointed to committee to investigate operations of
                    the Bank of the United States. Conducted investiga-
                    tion in Virginia area during Christmas recess.

                              1819
February 1   Spoke against Jackson's actions in invading Florida
                    and executing Arbuthnot and Ambrister.

February 20   Presented states' rights view of unconstitutionality
                    of the Bank of the United States in lengthy speech
                    in House.

April 29   Son, John, Jr., born.

                              1820
February 17   Spoke against any restrictions or limitations on the
                    admission of Missouri to the Union with full right
                    to determine her own internal institutions (slavery).

April 24   Opposed tariff increases and the "American System"
                    in the House.

                              1821
January 15   Resigned from Congress giving both the state of
                    his health and disappointment over the direction in
                    which the national legislature was moving as rea-
                    sons.

May 11   Daughter, Letitia, born.

1822

June   Fought with Col. John Macon over an alleged insult by Tyler to Macon in a court case. Macon slashed with whip.

1823

April   Elected to old seat in Virginia House of Delegates. Seated in December.

July 11   Daughter, Elizabeth, born.

1824

Appointed to the Board of Visitors of William and Mary College. Served on the Board until his death.

December 1   Electoral college met and gave Jackson 99 votes, Adams 84, Crawford 41 and Clay 37. Tyler had supported Crawford until his stroke and then John Quincy Adams as the least of the three remaining evils.

1825

March   Wrote letter to Clay congratulating him on his appointment as Secretary of State by President Adams.

April   Daughter, Anne Contesse, born. Lived only three months.

December 6   Disturbed by program of action for the national government which he saw in President Adams' first Annual Message.

December 10   Elected Governor of Virginia by the state legislature. Term was one year. The position had much prestige but little power.

1826

July 11   As governor and a great admirer of Jefferson he delivered an oration eulogizing him at ceremonies in Richmond.

December 4   Delivered Annual Message to the legislature in which he advocated internal improvements to promote travel between the eastern and western parts of the state and reorganization of the state's educational system.

December 10   Reelected as governor with only two votes cast a-
                gainst him.

1827

January 13   Elected United States Senator by Virginia legis-
                lature following bitter dispute over replacing John
                Randolph in that office. Resigned as governor but did
                not take seat in Senate until opening of new session
                in December.

March 23   Daughter, Alice, born.

UNITED STATES SENATOR AND CANDIDATE FOR THE VICE-PRESIDENCY

1828

Ill in early part of the year.

February 4   Gave first speech in the Senate in which he opposed
                federal involvement in internal improvements.

May 13   Voted against the Tariff of 1828.

November   Jackson and Calhoun, whom Tyler had supported,
                again as the lesser of two evils, defeated Adams
                and Rush for the presidency and vice-presidency.

1829

Again ill in the early part of the year. Then moved
from "Greenway," the estate on which he had been
raised, to new plantation, "Gloucester Place."

October 5   Virginia Convention to draft a new Constitution met.
                Tyler was an elected delegate but was not one of
                the most outspoken members. He took a moderate
                position and spoke in favor of concessions that
                would bind the eastern and western sections togeth-
                er. He usually voted with the more conservative
                eastern group.

1830

January 15   Work of the Virginia convention completed.

May 10   Spoke against confirmation of journalists appointed
                to federal offices by Jackson.

May 12   Spoke against federal involvement in the construction
                  of the Maysville, Washington, Paris, and Lexington
                  Turnpike. Led to speak, in part, by statements Clay
                  had made which Tyler considered insulting to Vir-
                  ginia.

May 27   Maysville Road bill vetoed by Jackson. Tyler's
                  enthusiasm for Jackson increased.

December 6   Son, Tazewell, born.

                                    1831
February   Opposed Jackson's recess appointments as infringing
                  on the powers of the Senate.

                                    1832
February 9   Delivered a two day speech opposing the proposed
  and 10   tariff bill (Tariff of 1832) on the grounds that while
                  it lowered rates it was still a protectionist measure
                  and thus an unjustified exercise of power by the
                  federal government.

June 9   Voted against the rechartering of the Bank of the
                  United States after expressing continued conviction
                  that it was unconstitutional.

July 10   Jackson vetoed rechartering of the Bank. This was
                  an important factor in Tyler's decision to support
                  him for reelection.

November 6   Jackson and Van Buren elected.

November 24   Tariff of 1832 nullified by South Carolina conven-
                  tion. This began a period of distress for Tyler who
                  supported states' rights and opposed the tariff but
                  rejected the right of nullification.

December 10   Andrew Jackson issued his "Proclamation to the
                  People of South Carolina."

December 28   Calhoun resigned Vice Presidency to accept Senate
                  seat left vacant when Hayne accepted the governor-
                  ship of South Carolina.

                                    1833
January   Tyler urged Clay to propose a compromise to end
                  the crisis.

January 16   Jackson requested congressional approval of the use of troops if necessary to compel South Carolina to obey the law.

January 26   Virginia legislature accepted as its own Tyler's position that a state had a right to secede but not to nullify a law and yet remain in the union. Further, that the federal government had no right to resort to arms even if a state did improperly nullify a federal law.

February 2   Tyler noted his fears of a coming "military despotism" in a letter to friend Littleton W. Tazewell. Had moved to a position of strong opposition to Jackson.

February 6   Spoke in Senate against the Force Bill. Saw restoration of mutual confidence among the states as the only means of preventing dissolution of the union.

February 12   Compromise tariff bill introduced by Clay.

February 20   Tyler cast the lone vote in the Senate against the Force Bill which passed 32 to 1.

March 1   Compromise tariff, already passed by House, passed by Senate with Tyler voting for it.

March 4   Reelected to Senate.

September   Jackson began removal of funds from the Bank of the United States.

                                1834
February 24   Spoke in Senate against withdrawal of funds maintaining that the veto had spelled the ultimate doom of the Bank and that withdrawal was both unnecessary and an infringement on the rights of those to whom the Bank had financial obligations. Expressed suspicion that funds withdrawn would be used for political purposes. In the speach he denied publicly that he belonged to the "Republican" (Jacksonian) party and spoke of his own "Whig principles." He also spoke well of his old rival, Henry Clay.

March 28   Voted in favor of censure of Jackson for withdrawal. Benton pledged to have censure expunged.

Spring   Involved in steps taken to form Whig Party bringing all Jackson foes including Anti-Masons, Southern states' rights Democrats, National Republicans, and supporters of Clay, together.

1835

December   Maryland Whig convention nominated ticket of Harrison and Tyler as part of the plan of dividing the vote among regional candidates and throwing the election into the House. Francis Granger of New York had been nominated for vice president with Harrison by Whig and Anti-Mason conventions in Pennsylvania and Indiana but Maryland had sought a running mate untainted by suspicions of abolitionism. Tyler subsequently nominated as running mate for Judge Hugh L. White by Virginia, Tennessee, North Carolina and Georgia Whigs.

1836

February 10   Virginia General Assembly passed Watkins Resolution instructing Senators Tyler and Leigh to vote in favor of the expunction of the censure of Jackson.

February 29   Resigned Senate seat rather than follow instructions and vote for expunction which he strenuously opposed. Felt he could not disobey instructions and retain seat, as Leigh did, in part because of his role in the condemnation of Brent and Giles for the same act in 1812.

December 7   Received 47 electoral votes for vice-president to Richard M. Johnson's 147, Granger's 77 and William Smith's 23. Election of vice-president sent to Senate for only time in history since no candidate received a majority.

1837

February 8   Senate chose Johnson over Granger for vice-president by vote of 33 to 16.

1838

January 10   Elected President of the Virginia Colonization Society. Spoke praising work of the Society in returning free Negroes to Africa but insisting that all such activities should be conducted on a state level with no interference from outside.

April 26   Elected as Whig to Virginia House of Delegates.

1839

January   Served briefly as Speaker of the House of Delegates.

February 23   Election of a senator postponed by Virginia House of Delegates. Whigs were divided between Tyler and William C. Rives who had Clay's support.

September   Virginia Whigs selected Clay and Nathaniel P. Talmadge as their presidential candidates.

December 4   Democratic Whig National Convention met at Harrisburg. Tyler, as part of the Virginia delegation, supported Clay. William Henry Harrison nominated on second ballot. Tyler nominated for vice-president with Virginia delegation abstaining.

1840

October   Made only speaking tour of campaign, traveling through western Pennsylvania and Kentucky.

December 2   Received 234 electoral votes for vice-president to 48 for Johnson.

1841

February 9   Arrived in Washington. Did not become involved in the selection of the cabinet.

VICE-PRESIDENT AND PRESIDENT

March 4   Inaugurated Vice-President of the United States. Delivered five-minute address.

April 4   President Harrison died after brief illness. Tyler in Williamsburg. Fletcher Webster sent by Secretary of State Daniel Webster to notify him.

April 5   Left for Washington almost immediately upon notification of Harrison's death.

April 6   Reached Washington at 4 A.M. Took oath of office at noon. Met with Harrison's cabinet and made decision to retain them as his own. Had, therefore, no supporters of his own in the cabinet.

April 9

Delivered Inaugural Address in which he spoke of a new test of the Constitution in the devolution of the "Presidential Office" upon him. Showed no doubt that he was President and not Acting President.

June 1

Addressed the special session of Congress called by Harrison. Spoke primarily of financial matters and asked Congress to devise a plan for a new financial system that would be constitution.

June 7

Henry Clay submitted a legislative program in resolution form. Although it was in agreement with the points in Tyler's special session message the Democrats tried to use it to drive a wedge between Clay and Tyler by calling it an attempt by the former to take leadership away from the President.

August 16

Vetoed compromise Fiscal Bank Bill passed by Congress August 6.

September 9

Vetoed Fiscal Corporation Bill which Whigs thought would be satisfactory to him.

September 11

All cabinet members except Webster who was involved in negotiations with Ashburton resigned. Webster remained in office until May 8, 1843.

September 13

Repudiated by Whig congressional caucus and declared expelled from the party.

October 11

Wrote to Webster suggesting that the annexation of Texas would throw a bright lustre around the administration but recognizing northern objections to it on anti-slavery grounds.

December 7

Delivered first Annual Message proposing an "Exchequer Plan," an increase in the revenue tariff and an expansion of the army and navy.

1842

March 25

Submitted message to Congress decrying continued deficit of the government and calling for upward revision of selected tariff duties in such a way as to increase revenue and encourage manufacturing. Noting that such a revision would cause suspension of the distribution of the proceeds from land sales to the states, he said that although he had supported distribution when passed because he thought there would be a surplus he could not consider it justified in times of deficit.

June 25   Congress passed a provisional tariff act to delay the rate reductions that would otherwise have taken place July 1 in conformity with the Compromise Tariff of 1833. The provisional act also called for the continuation of distribution and, because of this, Tyler vetoed it.

Summer   Concerned about Dorr's "People's Constitution" uprising in Rhode Island. Sent Secretary of War to that state and threatened to use federal troops if necessary. State militia under Governor King successfully routed Dorr's forces without federal intervention.

August 9   Vetoed permanent tariff bill which contained provisions similar to provisional one on the grounds that he would accept high tariff rates only if absolutely necessary to meet government revenue needs. Continuing distribution, he argued, caused the rates to be higher than they had to be. He called for a smaller rate increase and discontinuation of distribution.

August 11   Submitted Webster–Ashburton Treaty, signed August 9, to Senate.

August 16   Attacked in report by special committee headed by John Quincy Adams appointed to study his tariff veto message.

August 24   Letter from Webster to the President acknowledged Tyler's contribution to the success of the treaty negotiations.

August 30   Sent protest to House calling committee report it had accepted unfair and an infringement on the powers of the executive. Signed more moderate tariff increase bill which met the criteria laid down in his veto messages.

September 10   Wife, Letitia Christian Tyler, died.

October 19   Commodore Thomas Jones, believing that Mexico and the United States were at war, occupied Monterey, California, without firing a shot. Apologized, saluted the Mexican flag and departed when convinced of his error.

November	Tyler interpreted gains made by Democrats in midterm elections as evidence of popular support for his position on the bank question.
December 6	Delivered second Annual Message in which he expressed satisfaction over the Webster-Ashburton Treaty but noted that British actions to suppress the slave trade were still a matter of concern. He repeated his call for reform of the tariff structure and the creation of a constitutional fiscal institution.

1843

January 10	Resolution introduced by Representative John M. Botts calling for the establishment of a committee to prepare impeachment charges against Tyler defeated in the House.
May to September	A number of opponents removed from office and replaced by supporters. Critics called it a purge and accused Tyler of removing Whigs who had made his election possible and putting Democrats who found it expedient to support him at that moment in their places.
June 8	Left Washington for only prolonged trip during his presidency, one to Boston for ceremonies marking completion of the Bunker Hill Monument. Ceremonies held June 17.
December 5	Delivered third Annual Message in which he emphasized concern over whatever related to the Republic of Texas. His calls for tariff and fiscal reform were womewhat blunted by recognition that the country was doing well financially even without them.

1844

February 28	Naval gun "Peacemaker" exploded while presidential party was aboard "U.S.S. Princeton" for demonstration of it. Secretaries of State (Abel P. Upshur) and Navy killed. Also killed was former State Senator David Gardiner of New York, father of Julia Gardiner of whom Tyler had become enamored.
March 23	House resolution asked President for information regarding his actions in the Rhode Island crisis in the summer of 1842.

April 27	Submitted treaty with Texas for annexation to Senate. Negotiations had been completed April 12 by new Secretary of State Calhoun.
May 15	Dispatched forces to the Gulf of Mexico and Texas border to defend that Republic in the event that Mexico renewed hostilities while the treaty was being considered.
May 28	James K. Polk nominated by Democratic Convention meeting in Baltimore.
May 30	Tyler accepted nomination for reelection by Democratic-Republican Convention, a coalition of Tyler supporters, also meeting in Baltimore.
June 8	Treaty for annexation of Texas defeated in Senate 35 to 16.
June 10	Submitted all correspondence and documents relating to annexation of Texas to the House along with a message regretting the Senate's action and noting that the same objective could be accomplished in other ways by Congress.
June 17	Caleb Cushing, earlier rejected by Senate when nominated to be Secretary of the Treasury, approved as minister to negotiate treaty with China.
June 26	Married Julia Gardiner in quiet wedding because of recent death of her father.
July	Negotiations conducted for withdrawal of Tyler and his support of Polk in exchange for assurance of a strong position on Texas annexation and protection for Tylerite officeholders. Letter from Andrew Jackson outlining the terms was a key move in the negotiations.
August 20	Withdrew from presidential race.
December 3	Delivered fourth Annual Message in which he emphasized need for prompt action to annex Republic of Texas.
December 4	James K. Polk and George M. Dallas, Democrats, chosen with 170 electoral votes to 105 for Whigs Clay and Theodore Freylinghuysen.

December 18   Sent a strong letter to the House and Senate with
               dispatches showing the hostility of Mexico toward
               Texas and the United States, citing alleged barbaric
               acts by Mexicans and telling of Mexican attempts
               to turn the North against the South. He called for
               annexation and said that if hostilities resulted Mexico
               would bear full responsibility.

                                 1845
January 22   Submitted treaty with China to the Senate.

January 25   Tyler supported Joint Resolution for annexation of
               Texas passed by House 120 to 98.

February 27   Joint Resolution approved by Senate 27 to 25.

March 1   Annexation document signed by Tyler.

SOUTHERN PLANTER AND MODERATE
BECOME SECESSIONIST

March 4   James K. Polk inaugurated as 11th President of the
               United States. Early commentaries on Tyler stated
               that he failed to participate and attempted to leave
               Washington before the ceremony. Chitwood insists
               research shows this was a falsehood made up by
               Tyler's enemies and that Tyler rode in same car-
               riage with Polk. Apparently passed up inauguration
               ball but not inauguration itself.

March 5   Left Washington for new plantation in Virginia,
               "Sherwood Forest."

                                 1846
April 24   Mexican troops crossed Rio Grande to meet Ameri-
               can troops who had crossed the Nueces. War began.
               Tyler supported the war as a just one.

May   Appeared as a witness before the House Foreign
               Affairs Committee to refute charges made by Rep-
               resentative Charles Ingersoll that Daniel Webster
               had used Secret Service funds for his own benefit
               at the time that the Webster-Ashburton Treaty was
               being negotiated.

July 12   Son, David Gardiner Tyler, born.

August   Opposed acceptance of the Wilmot Proviso.

October   On receipt of reports of rich stores of coal on
                  land he owned in Kentucky, began a series of
                  costly and futile efforts, most of them in partner-
                  ship with brother-in-law, Alexander Gardiner, to
                  extract and sell it. Efforts finally abandonned in
                  1853.

                              1847
February 24   John C. Calhoun claimed to be the primary author
                  of the annexation of Texas. Tyler, believing that
                  honor was his, denied Calhoun's claims.

                              1848
April 7   Son, John Alexander Tyler, born.

                              1849
December 25   Daughter, Julia Gardiner Tyler, born.

                              1850
May   After considerable hesitation and doubt finally en-
                  dorsed the proposed compromise of 1850 Omnibus
                  Bill. Measure passed in September.

                              1851
December 2   Son, Lachlan Tyler, born.

                              1852
Spring   Suffered from pneumonia.

Summer   Supported Pierce against Scott.

                              1853
January 28   Article by Julia Gardiner Tyler responding to charges
                  by a group of British ladies, defended the right of
                  America to arrange its own institutions (slavery)
                  without British interference. Printed in the Rich-
                  mond "Enquirer."

August 24   Son, Lyon Gardiner Tyler, born.

1854

Supported Kansas-Nebraska Act. Attacked Know-Nothings for their opposition to the Roman Catholic Church. Expressed approval of that Church's non-involvement in the slavery issue in contrast to the Protestant denominations which were being split over the issue.

1855

January

Indicated his willingness to head a peace commission to Europe to help end the Crimean War if asked. Was not asked.

March 20

Delivered address in Baltimore encouraging all to heal old wounds and reunite. Sought to set example by treating old enemies, especially Henry Clay, with magnanimity.

1856

March 12

Son, Robert Fitzwalter Tyler, born.

April 24

Spoke at Petersburg and again called for an end to all animosities.

Summer

Supported Buchanan without any special enthusiasm for him but with great fear for the fate of the Union in the event of a Black Republican Fremont victory.

Winter

Seriously ill.

1857

Spring

Convinced of the need for a moderate Southerner in office, entertained some hope of being the Democratic nominee in 1860.

October 16

John Brown's raid aroused fears of slave uprisings in Tyler and his neighbors.

1860

April 12

Withdrew himself from any consideration as potential candidate for the Democratic nomination.

June 20

Daughter, Pearl Tyler, born.

Summer

Worked in Virginia to promote a Breckenridge-Douglas fusion ticket to heal wounds of Democratic

Party. Supported Breckenridge when this approved impossible.

December 5   Lincoln and Hannibal Hamlin received 180 electoral votes to 72 for Breckenridge, 39 for Bell and 12 for Douglas.

December 14   Tyler proposed conference of the 12 border states to seek a peaceful resolution of the crisis.

December 20   South Carolina seceeded.

1861

January 17   Peace convention called by the Virginia legislature. While Tyler was a moving force behind this, the convention call issued differed from the one he wanted in that it invited all states to send delegates rather than just the border states. Tyler had felt that the border states could represent all points of view in milder form and would be the ones most interested in finding a fair solution.

January 19   Appointed delegate from Virginia to the peace convention and also special commissioner to attempt to persuade President Buchanan to refrain from hostile actions pending the outcome of the convention.

January 24   Met with Buchanan.

January 28   Buchanan, as requested by Tyler, sent the Virginia call for a peace convention to Congress and announced that he would refrain from hostile acts.

February 5   Unanimously elected president of the peace convention meeting in Washington. Delivered keynote address which emphasized the part men from each state had played in creating the union and calling on all to help preserve it.

February 23   Led delegation from peace convention for interview with Lincoln. Results not satisfactory to Southerners.

February 25   Supported radical Southern position, as embodied in the Seddon amendment, at the convention. Amendment failed of adoption.

February 28   Back in Richmond, denounced results of the convention as unsatisfactory for the South. Called for secession by Virginia.

April 12   Fort Sumter fired on.

April 17   Special Virginia convention, with Tyler as member, voted secession.

Summer   Served as Register of the Treasury of the Confederacy.

November   Chosen to the Confederate House of Representatives.

1862

January 12   Became ill.

January 18   Died. Buried January 20.

INAUGURAL ADDRESS

April 9, 1841

*Tyler delivered his inaugural address three days after as-
suming the presidency on the death of Harrison. In contrast with Harrison's lengthy address, Tyler's was brief
and matter of fact. With the exception of brief comments on
the need for financial reform, he emphasized the kind of
government he would head rather than any policies he
would adopt. While others may have had doubts as to
whether he had assumed the presidential office or merely
the powers and duties of the president, Tyler made it clear
in the address as he did in his actions that it was the office as far as he was concerned.*

*Tyler had thought of following Harrison's example in his
Inaugural and declaring that he would not run again in
1844 but was persuaded not to do so by Duff Green.*

Washington, April 9, 1841

To the People of the United States.

FELLOW-CITIZENS: Before my arrival at the seat of Government
the painful communication was made to you by the officers presiding
over the several Departments of the deeply regretted death of William
Henry Harrison, late President of the United States. Upon him you
had conferred your suffrages for the first office in your gift, and had
selected him as your chosen instrument to correct and reform all
such errors and abuses as had manifested themselves from time to
time in the practical operation of the Government. While standing at
the threshold of this great work he has by the dispensation of an all-
wise Providence been removed from amongst us, and by the provisions
of the Constitution the efforts to be directed to the accomplishing of
this vitally important task have develed upon myself. This same oc-
currence has subjected the wisdom and sufficiency of our institutions to a new test. For the first time in our history the person elected to the Vice-Presidency of the United States, by the happening of a
contingency provided for in the Constitution, has had devolved upon
him the Presidential office. The spirit of faction, which is directly
opposed to the spirit of a lofty patriotism, may find in this occasion
for assaults upon my Administration; and in succeeding, under cir-

cumstances so sudden and unexpected and to responsibilities so greatly augmented, to the administration of public affairs I shall place in the intelligence and patriotism of the people my only sure reliance. My earnest prayer shall be constantly addressed to the all-wise and all-powerful Being who made me, and by whose dispensation I am called to the high office of President of the Confederacy, understandingly to carry out the principles of that Constitution which I have sworn "to protect, preserve, and defend."

The usual opportunity which is afforded to a Chief Magistrate upon his induction to office of presenting to his countrymen an exposition of the policy which would guide his Administration, in the form of an inaugural address, not having, under the peculiar circumstances which have brought me to the discharge of the high duties of President of the United States, been afforded to me, a brief exposition of the principles which will govern me in the general course of my administration of public affairs would seem to be due as well to myself as to you.

In regard to foreign nations, the groundwork of my policy will be justice on our part to all, submitting to injustice from none. While I shall sedulously cultivate the relations of peace and amity with one and all, it will be my most imperative duty to see that the honor of the country shall sustain no blemish. With a view to this, the condition of our military defenses will become a matter of anxious solicitude. The Army, which has in other days covered itself with renown, and the Navy, not inappropriately termed the right arm of the public defense, which has spread a light of glory over the American standard in all the waters of the earth, should be rendered replete with efficiency.

In view of the fact, well avouched by history, that the tendency of all human institutions is to concentrate power in the hands of a single man, and that their ultimate downfall has proceeded from this cause, I deem it of the most essential importance that a complete separation should take place between the sword and the purse. No matter where or how the public moneys shall be deposited, so long as the President can exert the power of appointing and removing at his pleasure the agents selected for their custody the Commander in Chief of the Army and Navy is in fact the treasurer. A permanent and radical change should therefore be decreed. The patronage incident to the Presidential office, already great, is constantly increasing. Such increase is destined to keep pace with the growth of our population, until, without a figure of speech, an army of officeholders may be spread over the land. The unrestrained power exerted by a selfishly ambitious man in order either to perpetuate his authority or to hand it over to some favorite as his successor may lead to the employment of all the means within his control to accomplish his object. The right to remove from office, while subjected to no just restraint, is inevitably destined to produce a spirit of crouching servility with the official corps, which, in order to uphold the hand which feeds them, would lead to direct and active interference in the ejections, both State and Federal, thereby subjecting the course of State legislation to the dictation of the chief executive officer and making the will of that officer absolute and supreme. I will at a proper time invoke the action of Congress upon this subject, and shall readily acquiesce in the adoption of all proper measures which are calculated to arrest these evils, so full of danger in their tendency. I will remove no incumbent from office who has faithfully and honestly acquitted himself of the duties of his office, except in such cases where such officer has been guilty of an active partisanship or by secret means — the less manly, and therefore the more objectionable — has given his official influence to the purposes of party, thereby bringing the patronage of the Government in conflict with the freedom of elections. Numerous removals may become necessary under this rule. These will be made by me through no acerbity of feeling — I have had no cause to cherish or indulge unkind feelings toward any — but my conduct will be regulated by a profound sense of what is due to the country and its institutions; nor shall I neglect to apply the same unbending rule to those of my own appointment. Freedom of opinion will be tolerated, the full enjoyment of the right of suffrage will be maintained as the birthright of every American citizen; but I say emphatically to the official corps, "Thus far and no farther." I have dwelt the longer upon this subject because removals from office are likely often to arise, and I would have my countrymen to understand the principle of the Executive action.

In all public expenditures the most rigid economy should be resorted to, and, as one of its results, a public debt in time of peace be sedulously avoided. A wise and patriotic constituency will never object to the imposition of necessary burdens for useful ends, and true wisdom dictates the resort to such means in order to supply deficiencies in the revenue, rather than to those doubtful expedients which, ultimating in a public debt, serve to embarrass the resources of the country and to lessen its ability to meet any great emergency which may arise. All sinecures should be abolished. The appropriations should be direct and explicit, so as to leave as limited a share of discretion to the disbursing agents as may be found compatible with the public service. A strict responsibility on the part of all the agents of the Government should be maintained and peculation or defalcation visited with immediate expulsion from office and the most condign punishment.

The public interest also demands that if any war has existed between the Government and the currency it shall cease. Measures of a financial character now having the sanction of legal enactment shall be faithfully enforced until repealed by the legislative authority. But I owe it to myself to declare that I regard existing enactments as unwise and impolitic and in a high degree oppressive. I shall promptly give my sanction to any constitutional measure which, originating in Congress, shall have for its object the restoration of a sound circulating medium, so essentially necessary to give confidence in all the transactions of life, to secure to industry its just and adequate rewards, and to reestablish the public prosperity. In deciding upon the adaptation of any such measure to the end proposed, as well as its conformity to the Constitution, I shall resort to the fathers of the great republican school for advice and instruction, to be drawn from their sage view of our system of government and the light of their ever-glorious example.

The institutions under which we live, my countrymen, secure each person in the perfect enjoyment of all his rights. The spectacle is exhibited to the world of a government deriving its powers from the consent of the governed and having imparted to it only so much power as is necessary for its successful operation. Those who are charged with its administration should carefully abstain from all attempts to enlarge the range of powers thus granted to the several departments of the Government other than by an appeal to the people for additional grants, lest by so doing they disturb that balance which the patriots and statesmen who framed the Constitution designed to establish between the Federal Government and the States composing the Union. The observance of these rules is enjoined upon us by that feeling of reverence and affection which finds a place in the heart of every patriot for the preservation of union and the blessings of union — for the good of our children and our children's children through countless generations. An opposite course could not fail to generate factions intent upon the gratification of their selfish ends, to give birth to local and sectional jealousies, and to ultimate either in breaking asunder the bonds of union or in building up a central system which inevitably end in a bloody scepter and an iron crown.

In conclusion I beg you to be assured that I shall exert myself to carry the foregoing principles into practice during my administration of the Government, and, confiding in the protecting care of an ever-watchful and overruling Providence, it shall be my first and highest duty to preserve unimpaired the free institutions under which we live and transmit them to those who shall succeed me in their full force and vigor.

SPECIAL SESSION MESSAGE

June 1, 1841

One of the few acts which William Henry Harrison was able to perform during his brief tenure as President was the calling of a special session of Congress to meet May 31, 1841, to consider ways to escape from the financial situation in which the country found itself. Tyler had become President by the time Congress had assembled and he addressed the special session.

As a defender of states' rights, Tyler had opposed the Banks of the United States. At the same time, as one who recognized the need for a strong currency in adequate supply and capable of circulating throughout the country, he was disturbed by the actions of Jackson and Van Buren which he saw as giving state banks the power to create limitless quantities of currency of questionable value.

The problem of developing a federal institution capable of doing the job and yet not infringing on state powers dominated the address to the special session as it did most of his major messages in the first half of his term. His attempt to find a solution were complicated by his view of the presidency which precluded his openly submitting and fighting for a definite plan of his own.

His special session message began with a brief review of the circumstances of his accession to office and of American foreign relations. It ended with a review of Indian and military affairs. In between he dwelt at length on fiscal matters. After estimating the probable deficit of the government as of September 1, 1841, at $4,845,000, he continued:

In order to supply the wants of the Government, an intelligent constituency, in view of their best interests, will without hesitation submit to all necessary burthens. But it is nevertheless important so to impose them as to avoid defeating the just expectations of the country growing out of preexisting laws. The act of the 2d of March, 1833, commonly called the "compromise act," should not be altered except under urgent necessities, which are not believed at this time to exist. One year only remains to complete the series of reductions provided for by that law, at which time provisions made by the same law, and which then will be brought actively in aid of the manufacturing interests of the Union, will not fail to produce the most beneficial results. Under a system of discriminating duties imposed for purposes of revenue, in unison with the provisions of existing laws, it is to be hoped that our policy will in the future be fixed and permanent, so as

to avoid those constant fluctuations which defeat the very objects
they have in view. We shall thus best maintain a position which, while
it will enable us the more readily to meet the advances of other countries calculated to promote our trade and commerce, will at the same
time leave in our own hands the means of retaliating with greater
effect unjust regulations.

In intimate connection with the question of revenue is that which
makes provision for a suitable fiscal agent, capable of adding increased
facilities in the collection and disbursement of the public revenues,
rendering more secure their custody, and consulting a true economy
in the great, multiplied, and delicate operations of the Treasury Department. Upon such an agent depends in an eminent degree the establishment of a currency of uniform value, which is of so great importance to all the essential interests of society, and on the wisdom to be
manifested in its creation much depends. So intimately interwoven are
its operations, not only with the interests of individuals, but of States,
that it may be regarded to a great degree as controlling both. If paper
be used as the chief medium of circulation, and the power be vested
in the Government of issuing it at pleasure, either in the form of
Treasury drafts or any other, or if banks be used as the public depositories, with liberty to regard all surpluses from day to day as so
much added to their active capital, prices are exposed to constant
fluctuations and industry to severe suffering. In the one case political
considerations directed to party purposes may control, while excessive cupidity may prevail in the other. The public is thus constantly
liable to imposition. Expansions and contractions may follow each
other in rapid succession — the one engendering a reckless spirit of
adventure and speculation, which embraces States as well as individuals, the other causing a fall in prices and accomplishing an entire
change in the aspect of affairs. Stocks of all sorts rapidly decline, individuals are ruined, and States embarrassed even in their efforts to
meet with punctuality the interest on their debts. Such, unhappily, is
the condition of things now existing in the United States. These effects
may readily be traced to the causes above referred to. The public
revenues, being removed from the then Bank of the United States, under an order of a late President, were placed in selected State banks,
which, actuated by the double motive of conciliating the Government
and augmenting their profits to the greatest possible extent, enlarged
extravagantly their discounts, thus enabling all other existing banks to
do the same; large dividends were declared, which, stimulating the
cupidity of capitalists, caused a rush to be made to the legislatures
of the respective States for similar acts of incorporation, which by
many of the States, under a temporary infatuation, were readily granted, and thus the augmentation of the circulating medium, consisting
almost exclusively of paper, produced a most fatal delusion. An illus-
tration derived from the land sales of the period alluded to will serve
best to show the effect of the whole system. The average sales of the

public lands for a period of ten years prior to 1834 had not much exceeded $2,000,000 per annum. In 1834 they attained in round numbers to the amount of $6,000,000; in the succeeding year of 1835 they reached $16,000,000, and the next year of 1836 they amounted to the enormous sum of $25,000,000, thus crowding into the short space of three years upward of twenty-three years' purchase of the public domain. So apparent had become the necessity of arresting this course of things that the executive department assumed the highly questionable power of discriminating in the funds to be used in payment by different classes of public debtors — a discrimination which was doubtless designed to correct this most ruinous state of things by the exaction of specie in all payments for the public lands, but which could not at once arrest the tide which had so strongly set in. Hence the demands for specie became unceasing, and corresponding prostration rapidly ensued under the necessities created with the banks to curtail their discounts and thereby to reduce their circulation. I recur to these things with no disposition to censure preexisting Administrations of the Government, but simply in exemplification of the truth of the position which I have assumed. If, then, any fiscal agent which may be created shall be placed, without due restrictions, either in the hands of the administrators of the Government or those of private individuals, the temptation to abuse will prove to be resistless. Objects of political aggrandizement may seduce the first, and the promptings of a boundless cupidity will assail the last. Aided by the experience of the past, it will be the pleasure of Congress so to guard and fortify the public interests in the creation of any new agent as to place them, so far as human wisdom can accomplish it, on a footing of perfect security. Within a few years past three different schemes have been before the country. The charter of the Bank of the United States expired by its own limitations in 1836. An effort was made to renew it, which received the sanction of the two Houses of Congress, but the then President of the United States exercised his veto power and the measure was defeated. A regard to truth requires me to say that the President was fully sustained in the course he had taken by the popular voice. His successor to the chair of state unqualifiedly pronounced his opposition to any new charter of a similar institution, and not only the popular election which brought him into power, but the elections through much of his term, seemed clearly to indicate a concurrence with him in sentiment on the part of the people. After the public moneys were withdrawn from the United States Bank they were placed in deposit with the State banks, and the result of that policy has been before the country. To say nothing as to the question whether that experiment was made under propitious or adverse circumstances, it may safely be asserted that it did receive the unqualified condemnation of most of its early advocates, and, it is believed, was also condemned by the popular sentiment. The existing subtreasury system does not seem to stand in higher favor with the people, but has recently been condemned in a manner too plainly indicated to admit of a doubt.

Thus in the short period of eight years the popular voice may be regarded as having successively condemned each of the three schemes of finance to which I have adverted. As to the first, it was introduced at a time (1816) when the State banks, then comparatively few in number, had been forced to suspend specie payments by reason of the war which had previously prevailed with Great Britain. Whether if the United States Bank charter, which expired in 1811, had been renewed in due season it would have been enabled to continue specie payments during the war and the disastrous period to the commerce of the country which immediately succeeded is, to say the least, problematical, and whether the United States Bank of 1816 produced a restoration of specie payments or the same was accomplished through the instrumentality of other means was a matter of some difficulty at that time to determine. Certain it is that for the first years of the operation of that bank its course was as disastrous as for the greater part of its subsequent career it became eminently successful. As to the second, the experiment was tried with a redundant Treasury, which continued to increase until it seemed to be the part of wisdom to distribute the surplus revenue among the States, which, operating at the same time with the specie circular and the causes before adverted to, caused them to suspend specie payments and involved the country in the greatest embarrassment. And as to the third, if carried through all the stages of its transmutation from paper and specie to nothing but the precious metals, to say nothing of the insecurity of the public moneys, its injurious effects have been anticipated by the country in its unqualified condemnation. What is now to be regarded as the judgment of the American people on this whole subject I have no accurate means of determining but by appealing to their more immediate representatives. The late contest, which terminated in the election of General Harrison to the Presidency, was decided on principles well known and openly declared, and while the subtreasury received in the result the most decided condemnation, yet no other scheme of finance seemed to have been concurred in. To you, then, who have come more directly from the body of our common constituents, I submit the entire question, as best qualified to give a full exposition of their wishes and opinions. I shall be ready to concur with you in the adoption of such system as you may propose, reserving to myself the ultimate power of rejecting any measure which may, in my view of it, conflict with the Constitution or otherwise jeopardize the prosperity of the country — a power which I could not part with even if I would, but which I will not believe any act of yours will call into requisition.

I can not avoid recurring, in connection with this subject, to the necessity which exists for adopting some suitable measure whereby the unlimited creation of banks by the States may be corrected in future. Such result can be most readily achieved by the consent of the States, to be expressed in the form of a compact among themselves, which they can only enter into with the consent and approbation of this Government – a consent which might in the present emergency of the public demands justifiably be given by Congress in advance of any action by the States, as an inducement to such action, upon terms well defined by the act of tender. Such a measure, addressing itself to the calm reflection of the States, would find in the experience of the past and the condition of the present much to sustain it; and it is greatly to be doubted whether any scheme of finance can prove for any length of time successful while the States shall continue in the unrestrained exercise of the power of creating banking corporations. This power can only be limited by their consent.

With the adoption of a financial agency of a satisfactory character the hope may be indulged that the country may once more return to a state of prosperity. Measures auxiliary thereto, and in some measure inseparably connected with its success, will doubtless claim the attention of Congress. Among such a distribution of the proceeds of the sales of the public lands, provided such distribution does not force upon Congress the necessity of imposing upon commerce heavier burthens than those contemplated by the act of 1833, would act as an efficient remedial measure by being brought directly in aid of the States. As one sincerely devoted to the task of preserving a just balance in our system of Government by the maintenance of the States in a condition the most free and respectable and in the full possession of all their power, I can no otherwise than feel desirous for their emancipation from the situation to which the pressure on their finances now subjects them. And while I must repudiate, as a measure founded in error and wanting constitutional sanction, the slightest approach to an assumption by this Government of the debts of the States, yet I can see in the distribution adverted to much to recommend it. The compacts between the proprietor States and this Government expressly guarantee to the States all the benefits which may arise from the sales. The mode by which this to be effected addresses itself to the discretion of Congress as the trustee for the States, and its exercise after the most beneficial manner is restrained by nothing in the grants or in the Constitution so long as Congress shall consult that equality in the distribution which the compacts require. In the present condition of some of the States the question of distribution may be regarded as substantially a question between direct and indirect taxation. If the distribution be not made in some form or other, the necessity will daily become more urgent with the debtor States for a resort to an oppressive system of direct taxation, or their credit, and necessarily their power and influence, will be greatly diminshed. The payment of taxes after the most inconvenient and oppressive mode will be exacted in place of contributions for the most part voluntarily made, and therefore comparatively unoppressive. The States are emphatically the constituents of this Government, and we should be entirely regardless of the objects held in view by them in the creation of this Government if we could be indifferent to their good. The happy effects of such a measure upon all the States would immediately be manifested. With the debtor States it would effect the relief to a great extent of the citizens from a heavy burthen of direct taxation, which presses with severity on the laboring classes, and eminently assist in restoring the general prosperity. An immediate advance would take place in the price of the State securities, and the attitude of the States would become one more, as it should ever be, lofty and erect. With States laboring under no extreme pressure from debt, the fund which they would derive from this source would enable them to improve their condition in an eminent degree. So far as this Government is concerned, appropriations to domestic objects approaching in amount the revenue derived from the land sales might be abandoned, and thus a system of unequal, and therefore unjust, legislation would be substituted by one dispensing equality to all the members of this Confederacy. Whether such distribution should be made directly to the States in the proceeds of the sales or in the form of profits by virtue of the operations of any fiscal agency having those proceeds as its basis, should such measure be contemplated by Congress, would well deserve its consideration. Nor would such disposition of the proceeds of the sales in any manner prevent Congress from time to time from passing all necessary preemption laws for the benefit of actual settlers, or from making any new arrangement as to the price of the public lands which might in future be esteemed desirable.

VETO MESSAGES
August 16 and September 9, 1841

At the request of the Senate, Secretary of the Treasury Ewing submitted a proposal for a fiscal institution June 12. It called for a bank in the District of Columbia with branches in the states which consented to have them. In order to make the stock more attractive, a select committee under Clay modified the plan to make it call for a national bank with its central office in Washington and with the power to establish branches in the states without their consent. Knowing that Tyler would veto such a bill, a compromise proposed by John Minor Botts requiring state assent but assuming it unless explicitly denied, was adopted. With Whigs supporting and Democrats opposing, this was passed. Tyler vetoed it August 16.

A second bill, believed to be acceptable to the President, was then drafted and passed. It created a fiscal corporation which could establish branches in the states and deal in exchanges but denied it the right to discount notes. Tyler vetoed this measure as well on the grounds that unless limits were placed on the power to deal in exchanges, it could be used in exactly the same way as the power to discount. Banks which could do that, he insisted, had to be assented to by the states in which they were located.

In the August 16 veto message he began by explaining his understanding of the presidential veto power and then proceeded to the substance of the Bill being considered.

Without going further into the argument, I will say that in looking to the powers of this Government to collect, safely keep, and disburse the public revenue, and incidentally to regulate the commerce and exchanges, I have not been able to satisfy myself that the establishment by this Government of a bank of discount in the ordinary acceptation of that term was a necessary means or one demanded by propriety to execute those powers. What can the local discounts of the bank have to do with the collecting, safe-keeping, and disbursing of the revenue? So far as the mere discounting of paper is concerned, it is quite immaterial to this question whether the discount is obtained at a State bank or a United States bank. They are both equally local, both beginning and both ending in a local accommodation. What influence have local discounts granted by any form of bank in the regulating of the currency and the exchanges? Let the history of the late United States Bank aid us in answering this inquiry.

For several years after the establishment of that institution it dealt almost exclusively in local discounts, and during that period the country was for the most part disappointed in the consequences anticipated from its incorporation. A uniform currency was not provided, exchanges were not regulated, and little or nothing was added to the general circulation, and in 1820 its embarrassments had become so great that the directors petitioned Congress to repeal that article of the charter which made its notes receivable everywhere in payment of the public dues. It had up to that period dealt to but a very small extent in exchanges, either foreign or domestic, and as late as 1823 its operations in that line amounted to a little more than $7,000,000 per annum. A very rapid augmentation soon after occurred, and in 1833 its dealings in the exchanges amounted to upward of $100,000,000. including the sales of its own drafts; and all these immense transactions were effected without the employment of extraordinary means. The currency of the country became sound, and the negotiations in the exchanges were carried on at the lowest possible rates. The circulation was increased to more than $22,000,000 and the notes of the bank were regarded as equal to specie all over the country, thus showing almost conclusively that it was the capacity to deal in exchanges, and not in local discounts, which furnished these facilities and advantages. It may be remarked, too, that notwithstanding the immense transactions of the bank in the purchase of exchange, the losses sustained were merely nominal, while in the line of discounts the suspended debt was enormous and proved most disastrous to the bank and the country. Its power of local discount has in fact proved to be a fruitful source of favoritism and corruption, alike destructive to the public morals and to the general weal.

The capital invested in banks of discount in the United States, created by the States, at this time exceeds $350,000,000, and if the discounting of local paper could have produced any beneficial effects the United States ought to possess the soundest currency in the world; but the reverse is lamentably the fact.

Is the measure now under consideration of the objectionable character to which I have alluded? It is clearly so unless by the sixteenth fundamental article of the eleventh section it is made otherwise. That article is in the following words:

> The directors of the said corporation shall establish one competent office of discount and deposit in any State in which two thousand shares shall have been subscribed or may be held, whenever, upon application of the legislature of such State, Congress may by law require the same. And the said directors may also establish one or more competent offices of discount and deposit in any Territory or District of the United States, and in any State with the assent of such State, and when established the said office or offices shall be only withdrawn or removed by the said directors prior to the expiration of this charter with the

previous assent of Congress: <u>Provided,</u> In respect to any
State which shall not, at the first session of the legislature
thereof held after the passage of this act, by resolution or
other usual legislative proceeding, unconditionally assent
or dissent to the establishment of such office or offices
within it, such assent of the said State shall be thereafter
presumed: <u>And provided, nevertheless,</u> That whenever it
shall become necessary and proper for carrying into execution any of the powers granted by the Constitution to
establish an office or offices in any of the States whatever,
and the establishment thereof shall be directed by law, it
shall be the duty of the said directors to establish such
office or offices accordingly.

It will be seen that by this clause the directors are invested with
the fullest power to establish a branch in any State which has yielded
its assent; and having once established such branch, it shall not
afterwards be withdrawn except by order of Congress. Such assent is
to be <u>implied</u> and to have the force and sanction of an actually expressed assent, "provided, in respect to any State which shall not,
at <u>the first session</u> of the legislature thereof held after the passage
of this act, by <u>resolution or other usual legislative proceeding, un-</u>
<u>conditionally</u> assent or dissent to the establishment of such office or
offices within it, such assent of said State shall be thereafter presumed." The assent or dissent is to be expressed <u>unconditionally</u>
<u>at the first session of the legislature, by</u> some formal legislative
act; and if not so expressed its assent is to be <u>implied,</u> and the directors are thereupon invested with power, at such time thereafter as
they may please, to establish branches, which can not afterwards be
withdrawn except by resolve of Congress. No matter what may be
the cause which may operate with the legislature, which either pre-
vents it from speaking or addresses itself to its wisdom, to induce
delay, its assent is to be implied. This iron rule is to give way to no
circumstances; it is unbending and inflexible. It is the language of
the master to the vassal; an unconditional answer is claimed forth-
with, and delay, postponement, or incapacity to answer produces an
implied assent which is ever after irrevocable. Many of the State
elections have already taken place without any knowledge on the part
of the people that such a question was to come up. The representatives
may desire a submission of the question to their constituents prep-
atory to final action upon it, but this high privilege is denied; whatever may be the motives and views entertained by the representatives of the people to induce delay, their assent is to be presumed,
and is ever afterwards binding unless their dissent shall be unconditionally expressed at their first session after the passage of this
bill into a law. They may by formal resolution declare the question
of assent or dissent to be undecided and postponed, and yet, in opposition to their express declaration to the contrary, their assent is to be

implied. Cases innumerable might be cited to manifest the irration-
ality of such an inference. Let one or two in addition suffice. The popular branch of the legislature may express its dissent by an unani-
mous vote, and its resolution may be defeated by a tie vote of the
senate, and yet the assent is to be implied. Both branches of the legislature may concur in a resolution of decided dissent, and yet the governor may exert the veto power conferred on him by the State constitution, and their legislative action be defeated, and yet the assent of
the legislative authority is implied, and the directors of this contemplated institution are authorized to establish a branch or branches
in such State whenever they may find it conducive to the interest of
the stockholders to do so; and having once established it they can
under no circumstances withdraw it except by act of Congress. The
State may afterwards protest against such unjust inference, but its
authority is gone. Its assent is implied by its failure or inability to
act at its first session, and its voice can never afterwards be heard.
To inferences so violent and, as they seem to me, irrational I can not
yield my consent. No court of justice would or could sanction them
without reversing all that is established in judicial proceeding by introducing presumptions at variance with fact and inferences at the
expense of reason. A State in a condition of duress would be presumed
to speak as an individual manacled and in prison might be presumed
to be in the enjoyment of freedom. Far better to say to the States
boldly and frankly, Congress wills and submission is demanded.

It may be said that the directors may not establish branches under
such circumstances; but this is a question of power, and this bill in-
vests them with full authority to do so. If the legislature of New York
or Pennsylvania or any other State should be found to be in such condition as I have supposed, could there by any security furnished
against such a step on the part of the directors? Nay, is it not fairly
to be presumed that this proviso was introduced for the sole purpose
of meeting the contingency referred to? Why else should it have been
introduced? And I submit to the Senate whether it can be believed
that any State would be likely to sit quietly down under such a state
of things. In a great measure of public interest their patriotism may
be successfully appealed to, but to infer their assent from circumstances at war with such inference I can not but regard as calculated
to excite a feeling at fatal enmity with the peace and harmony of the
country. I must therefore regard this clause as asserting the power
to be in Congress to establish offices of discount in a State not only
without its assent, but against its dissent, and so regarding it I can
not sanction it. On general principles the right in Congress to prescribe terms to any State implies a superiority of power and control,
deprives the transaction of all pretense to compact between them, and
terminates as we have seen, in the total abrogation of freedom of
action on the part of the States. But, further, the State may express,
after the most solemn form of legislation, its dissent, which may from

time to time thereafter be repeated in full view of its own interest, which can never be separated from the wise and beneficent operation of this Government, and yet Congress may by virtue of the last proviso overrule its law, and upon grounds which to such State will appear to rest on a constructive necessity and propriety and nothing more. I regard the bill as asserting for Congress the right to incorporate a United States bank with power and right to establish offices of discount and deposit in the several States of this Union with or without their consent — a principle to which I have always heretofore been opposed and which can never obtain my sanction; and waiving all other considerations growing out of its other provisions, I return it to the House in which it originated with these my objections to its approval.

                                        JOHN TYLER

He explained his main objections to the second measure, the Fiscal Corporation bill, in the following manner in the second veto message:

When I come to look at the details of the bill, they do not recommend it strongly to my adoption. A brief notice of some of its provisions will suffice.

First. It may justify substantially a system of discounts of the most objectionable character. It is to deal in bills of exchange drawn in one State and payable in another without any restraint. The bill of exchange may have an unlimited time to run, and its renewability is nowhere guarded against. It may, in fact, assume the most objectionable form of accommodation paper. It is not required to rest on any actual, real, or substantial exchange basis. A drawer in one place becomes the accepter in another, and so in turn the accepter may become the drawer upon a mutual understanding. It may at the same time indulge in mere local discounts under the name of bills of exchange. A bill drawn at Philadelphia on Camden, N.J., at New York on a border town in New Jersey, at Cincinnati on Newport, in Kentucky, not to multiply other examples, might, for anything in this bill to restrain it, become a mere matter of local accommodation. Cities thus relatively situated would possess advantages over cities otherwise situated of so decided a character as most justly to excite dissatisfaction.

Second. There is no limit prescribed to the premium in the purchase of bills of exchange, thereby correcting none of the evils under which the community now labors, and operating most injuriously upon the agricultural States, in which the irregularities in the rates of exchange are most severely felt. Nor are these the only consequences. A resumption of specie payments by the banks of those States would be liable to indefinite postponement; for as the operation of the agencies of the interior would chiefly consist in selling bills of exchange, and the purchases could only be made in specie or the notes of banks paying specie, the State banks would either have to continue with their doors closed or exist at the mercy of this national monopoly of brokerage. Nor can it be passed over without remark that whilst the District of Columbia is made the seat of the principal bank, its citizens are excluded from all participation in any benefit it might afford by a positive prohibition on the bank from all discounting within the District.

These are some of the objections which prominently exist against the details of the bill. Others might be urged of much force, but it would be unprofitable to dwell upon them. Suffice it to add that this charter is designed to continue for twenty years without a competitor; that the defects to which I have alluded, being founded on the fundamental law of the corporation, are irrevocable, and that if the objections be well founded it would be overhazardous to pass the bill into a law.

In conclusion I take leave most respectfully to say that I have felt the most anxious solicitude to meet the wishes of Congress in the adoption of a fiscal agent which, avoiding all constitutional objections, should harmonize conflicting opinions. Actuated by this feeling, I have been ready to yield much in a spirit of conciliation to the opinions of others; and it is with great pain that I now feel compelled to differ from Congress a second time in the same session. At the commencement of this session, inclined from choice to defer to the legislative will, I submitted to Congress the propriety of adopting a fiscal agent which, without violating the Constitution, would separate the public money from the Executive control and perform the operations of the Treasury without being burdensome to the people or inconvenient or expensive to the Government. It is deeply to be regretted that this department of the Government can not upon constitutional and other grounds concur with the legislative department in this last measure proposed to attain these desirable objects.

*   *   *   *

JOHN TYLER

FIRST ANNUAL MESSAGE
December 7, 1841

*At the beginning of the Harrison-Tyler administration most
interest in foreign affairs was focused on relations with
Great Britain. Tension between the United States and
Great Britain was high as a result of the series of battles
along the border between Maine and Canada known as the
"Aroostook War" in 1839 and had been heightened further
in November, 1840, by the arrest of a British subject,
Alexander McLeod, for the death of an American named
Durfree killed during the burning of the steamer* Caroline
in December, 1837.

*The replacement of the fiery Lord Palmerston as British
Foreign Minister by the more moderate Lord Aberdeen had
made peaceful solution of the disputes more likely by the
time of this annual message, but a happy settlement was
far from certain in December, 1841.*

To the Senate and House of Representatives of the United States:

In coming together, fellow-citizens, to enter again upon the discharge of the duties with which the people have charged us severally,
we find great occasion to rejoice in the general prosperity of the
country. We are in the enjoyment of all the blessings of civil and
religious liberty, with unexampled means of education, knowledge, and
improvement. Through the year which is now drawing to a close peace
has been in our borders and plenty in our habitations, and although
disease has visited some few portions of the land with distress and
mortality, yet in general the health of the people has been preserved,
and we are all called upon by the highest obligations of duty to renew
our thanks and our devotion to our Heavenly Parent, who has continued to vouchsafe to us the eminent blessings which surround us and
who has so signally crowned the year with His goodness. If we find
ourselves increasing beyond example in numbers, in strength, in
wealth, in knowledge, in everything which promotes human and social
happiness, let us ever remember our dependence for all these on the
protection and merciful dispensations of Divine Providence.

Since your last adjournment Alexander McLeod, a British subject
who was indicted for the murder of an American citizen, and whose
case has been the subject of a correspondence heretofore communicated to you, has been acquitted by the verdict of an impartial and intelligent jury, and has under the judgment of the court been regularly
discharged.

Great Britain having made known to this Government that the expedition which was fitted out from Canada for the destruction of the steamboat Caroline in the winter of 1837, and which resulted in the destruction of said boat and in the death of an American citizen, was undertaken by orders emanating from the authorities of the British Government in Canada, and demanding the discharge of McLeod upon the ground that if engaged in that expedition he did but fulfill the orders of his Government, has thus been answered in the only way in which she could be answered by a government the powers of which are distributed among its several departments by the fundamental law. Happily for the people of Great Britain, as well as those of the United States, the only mode by which an individual arraigned for a criminal offense before the courts of either can obtain his discharge is by the independent action of the judiciary and by proceedings equally familiar to the courts of both countries.

If in Great Britain a power exists in the Crown to cause to be entered a nolle prosequi, which is not the case with the Executive power of the United States upon a prosecution pending in a State court, yet there no more than here can the chief executive power rescue a prisoner from custody without an order of the proper tribunal directing his discharge. The precise stage of the proceedings at which such order may be made is a matter of municipal regulation exclusively, and not to be complained of by any other government. In cases of this kind a government becomes politically responsible only when its tribunals of last resort are shown to have rendered unjust and injurious judgments in matters not doubtful. To the establishment and elucidation of this principle no nation has lent its authority more efficiently than Great Britain. Alexander McLeod, having his option either to prosecute a writ of error from the decision of the supreme court of New York, which had been rendered upon his application for a discharge, to the Supreme Court of the United States, or to submit his case to the decision of a jury, preferred the latter, deeming it the readiest mode of obtaining his liberation; and the result has fully sustained the wisdom of his choice. The manner in which the issue submitted was tried will satisfy the English Government that the principles of justice will never fail to govern the enlightened decision of an American tribunal. I can not fail, however, to suggest to Congress the propriety, and in some degree the necessity, of making such provisions by law, so far as they may constitutionally do so, for the removal at their commencement and at the option of the party of all such cases as may hereafter arise, and which may involve the faithful observance and execution of our international obligations, from the State to the Federal judiciary. This Government, by our institutions, is charged with the maintenance of peace and the preservation of amicable relations with the nations of the earth, and ought to possess without question all the reasonable and proper means of maintaining the one and preserving the other. While just confidence is felt in the judiciary of the States, yet this Government ought to be competent in itself for the fulfillment of the high duties which have been devolved upon it under the organic law by the States themselves.

In the month of September a party of armed men from Upper Canada invaded the territory of the United States and forcibly seized upon the person of one Grogan, and under circumstances of great harshness hurriedly carried him beyond the limits of the United States and delivered him up to the authorities of Upper Canada. His immediate discharge was ordered by those authorities upon the facts of the case being brought to their knowledge – a course of procedure which was to have been expected from a nation with whom we are at peace, and which was not more due to the rights of the United States than to its own regard for justice. The correspondence which passed between the Department of State and the British envoy, Mr. Fox, and with the governor of Vermont, as soon as the facts had been made known to this department, are herewith communicated.

I regret that it is not in my power to make known to you an equally satisfactory conclusion in the case of the Caroline steamer, with the circumstances connected with the destruction of which, in December, 1837, by an armed force fitted out in the Province of Upper Canada, you are already made acquainted. No such atonement as was due for the public wrong done to the United States by this invasion of her territory, so wholly irreconcilable with her rights as an independent power, has yet been made. In the view taken by this Government the inquiry whether the vessel was in the employment of those who were prosecuting an unauthorized war against that Province or was engaged by the owner in the business of transporting passengers to and from Navy Island in hopes of private gain, which was most probably the case, in no degree alters the real question at issue between the two Governments. This Government can never concede to any foreign government the power, except in a case of the most urgent and extreme necessity, of invading its territory, either to arrest the persons or destroy the property of those who may have violated the municipal laws of such foreign government or have disregarded their obligations arising under the law of nations. The territory of the United States must be regarded as sacredly secure against all such invasions until they shall voluntarily acknowledge their inability to acquit themselves of their duties to others. And in announcing this sentiment I do but affirm a principle which no nation on earth would be more ready to vindicate at all hazards than the people and Government of Great Britain. If upon a full investigation of all facts it shall appear that the owner of the Caroline was governed by a hostile intent or had made common cause with those who were in the occupancy of Navy Island, then so far as he is concerned there can be no claim to indemnity for the destruction of his boat which this Government would feel itself bound to prosecute, since he would have acted not only in derogation of the rights of Great Britain, but in clear violation of the

laws of the United States; but that is a question which, however settled, in no manner involves the higher consideration of the violation of
territorial sovereignty and jurisdiction. To recognize it as an admis-
sible practice that each Government in its turn, upon any sudden and
unauthorized outbreak which, on a frontier the extent of which renders
it impossible for either to have an efficient force on every mile of it,
and which outbreak, therefore, neither may be able to supress in a
day, may take vengeance into its own hands, and without even a remonstrance, and in the absence of any pressing or overruling necessity may invade the territory of the other, would inevitably lead to
results equally to be deplored by both. When border collisions come to
receive the sanction or to be made on the authority of either Government general war must be the inevitable result. While it is the ardent
desire of the United States to cultivate the relations of peace with all
nations and to fulfill all the duties of good neighborhood toward those
who possess territories adjoining their own, that very desire would
lead them to deny the right of any foreign power to invade their boundary with an armed force. The correspondence between the two
Governments on this subject will at a future day of your session be
submitted to your consideration; and in the meantime I can not but indulge the hope that the British Government will see the propriety
of renouncing as a rule of future action the precedent which has been
set in the affair at Schlosser.

I herewith submit the correspondence which has recently taken
place between the American minister at the Court of St. James, Mr.
Stevenson, and the minister of foreign affairs of that Government on
the right claimed by that Government to visit and detain vessels
sailing under the American flag and engaged in prosecuting lawful
commerce in the African seas. Our commercial interests in that
region have experienced considerable increase and have become an
object of much importance, and it is the duty of this Government to
protect them against all improper and vexatious interruption. However desirous the United States may be for the supression of the slave
trade, they can not consent to interpolations into the maritime code at
the mere will and pleasure of other governments. We deny the right
of any such interpolation to any one or all the nations of the earth
without our consent. We claim to have a voice in all amendments or
alterations of that code, and when we are given to understand, as in
this instance, by a foreign government that its treaties with other
nations can not be executed without the establishment and enforcement
of new principles of maritime police, to be applied without our consent, we must employ a language neither of equivocal import or susceptible of misconstruction. American citizens prosecuting a lawful
commerce in the African seas under the flag of their country are not
responsible for the abuse or unlawful use of that flag by others; nor
can they rightfully on account of any such alleged abuses be interrupted,
molested, or detained while on the ocean, and if thus molested and

detained while pursuing honest voyages in the usual way and violating no law themselves they are unquestionably entitled to indemnity. This Government has manifested its repugnance to the slave trade in a manner which can not be misunderstood. By its fundamental law it prescribed limits in point of time to its continuance, and against its own citizens who might so far forget the rights of humanity as to engage in that wicked traffic it has long since by its municipal laws denounced the most condign punishment. Many of the States composing this Union had made appeals to the civilized world for its suppression long before the moral sense of other nations had become shocked by the iniquities of the traffic. Whether this Government should now enter into treaties containing mutual stipulations upon this subject is a question for its mature deliberation. Certain it is that if the right to detain American ships on the high seas can be justified on the plea of a necessity for such detention arising out of the existence of treaties between other nations, the same plea may be extended and enlarged by the new stipulations of new treaties to which the United States may not be a party. This Government will not cease to urge upon that of Great Britain full and ample remuneration for all losses, whether arising from detention or otherwise, to which American citizens have heretofore been or may hereafter be subjected by the exercise of rights which this Government can not recognize as legitimate and proper. Nor will I indulge a doubt but that the sense of justice of Great Britain will constrain her to make retribution for any wrong or loss which any American citizen engaged in the prosecution of lawful commerce may have experienced at the hands of her cruisers or other public authorities. This Government, at the same time, will relax no effort to prevent its citizens, if there by any so disposed, from prosecuting a traffic so revolting to the feelings of humanity. It seeks to do no more than to protect the fair and honest trader from molestation and injury; but while the enterprising mariner engaged in the pursuit of an honorable trade is entitled to its protection, it will visit with condign punishment others of an opposite character.

I invite your attention to existing laws for the suppression of the African slave trade, and recommend all such alterations as may give to them greater force and efficacy. That the American flag is grossly abused by the abandoned and profligate of other nations is but too probable. Congress has not long since had this subject under its consideration, and its importance well justifies renewed and anxious attention.

I also communicate herewith the copy of a correspondence between Mr. Stevenson and Lord Palmerston upon the subject, so interesting to several of the Southern States, of the rice duties, which resulted honorably to the justice of Great Britain and advantageously to the United States.

At the opening of the last annual session the President informed Congress of the progress which had then been made in negotiating a

convention between this Government and that of England with a view
to the final settlement of the question of the boundary between the
territorial limits of the two countires. I regret to say that little further advancement of the object has been accomplished since last year,
but this is owing to circumstances no way indicative of any abate-
ment of the desire of both parties to hasten the negotiation to its conclusion and to settle the question in dispute as early as possible. In
the course of the session it is my hope to be able to announce some
further degree of progress toward the accomplishment of this highly
desirable end.

The commission appointed by this Government for the exploration
and survey of the line of boundary separating the States of Maine and
New Hampshire from the conterminous British Provinces is, it is
believed, about to close its field labors and is expected soon to report
the results of its examinations to the Department of State. The report,
when received, will be laid before Congress.

> *Tyler went on to mention a number of other matters of
> foreign affairs, notably the "deep interest" of the United
> States in the young but growing Republic of Texas. He
> then turned to domestic issues.*

The Secretary of State, on whom the acts of Congress have devolved
the duty of directing the proceedings for the taking of the sixth census
or enumeration of the inhabitants of the United States, will report to
the two Houses the progress of that work. The enumeration of persons
has been completed, and exhibits a grand total of 17,069,453, making an
increase over the census of 1830 of 4,202,646 inhabitants, and showing
a gain in a ratio exceeding 32-1/2 per cent for the last ten years.

From the report of the Secretary of the Treasury you will be informed of the condition of the finances. The balance in the Treasury on
the 1st of January last, as stated in the report of the Secretary of the
Treasury submitted to Congress at the extra session, was $987,345.03.
The receipts into the Treasury during the first three quarters of this
year from all sources amount to $23,467,072.52; the estimated receipts
for the fourth quarter amount to $6,943,095.25, amounting to
$30,410,167.77, and making with the balance in the Treasury on the 1st
of January last $31,397,512.80. The expenditures for the first three
quarters of this year amount to $24,734,346.97. The expenditures for
the fourth quarter as estimated will amount to $7,290,723.73, thus
making a total of $32,025,070.70, and leaving a deficit to be provided
for on the 1st of January next of about $627,557.90.

Of the loan of $12,000,000 which was authorized by Congress at its
late session only $5,432,726.88 have been negotiated. The shortness of
time which it had to run has presented no inconsiderable impediment
in the way of its being taken by capitalists at home, while the same

cause would have operated with much greater force in the foreign market. For that reason the foreign market has not been resorted to; and it is now submitted whether it would not be advisable to amend the law by making what remains undisposed of payable at a more distant day.

Should it be necessary, in any view that Congress may take of the subject, to revise the existing tariff of duties, I beg leave to say that in the performance of that most delicate operation moderate counsels would seem to be the wisest. The Government under which it is our happiness to live owes its existence to the spirit of compromise which prevailed among its framers; jarring and discordant opinions could only have been reconciled by that noble spirit of patriotism which prompted conciliation and resulted in harmony. In the same spirit the compromise bill, as it is commonly called, was adopted at the session of 1833. While the people of no portion of the Union will ever hesitate to pay all necessary taxes for the support of Government, yet an innate repugnance exists to the imposition of burthens not really necessary for that object. In imposing duties, however, for the purposes of revenue a right to discriminate as to to the articles on which the duty shall be laid, as well as the amount, necessarily and most properly exists; otherwise the Government would be placed in the condition of having to levy the same duties upon all articles, the productive as well as the unproductive. The slightest duty upon some might have the effect of causing their importation to cease, whereas others, entering extensively into the consumption of the country, might bear the heaviest without any sensible diminution in the amount imported. So also the Government may be justified in so discriminating by reference to other considerations of domestic policy connected with our manufactures. So long as the duties shall be laid with distinct reference to the wants of the Treasury no well-formed objection can exist against them. It might be esteemed desirable that no such augumentation of the taxes should take place as would have the effect of annulling the land-proceeds distribution act of the last session, which act is declared to be inoperative the moment the duties are increased beyond 20 percent, the maximum rate established by the compromise act. Some of the provisions of the compromise act, which will go into effect on the 30th day of June next, may, however, be found exceedingly inconvenient in practice under any regulations that Congress may adopt. I refer more particularly to that relating to the home valuation. A difference in value of the same articles to some extent will necessarily exist at different ports, but that is altogether insignificant when compared with the conflicts in valuation which are likely to arise from the differences of opinion among the numerous appraisers of merchandise. In many instances the estimates of value must be conjectural, and thus as many different rates of value may be established as there are appraisers. These differences in valuation may also be increased by the inclination which, without the slightest impu-

tation on their honesty, may arise on the part of the appraisers in
favor of their respective ports of entry. I recommend this whole subject to the consideration of Congress with a single additional remark.
Certainty and permanency in any system of governmental policy are in
all respects eminently desirable, but more particularly is this true
in all that affects trade and commerce, the operations of which depend much more on the certainty of their returns and calculations
which embrace distant periods of time than on high bounties or duties,
which are liable to constant fluctuations.

At your late session I invited your attention to the condition of the
currency and exchanges and urged the necessity of adopting such
measures as were consistent with the constitutional competency of the
Government in order to correct the unsoundness of the one and, as
far as practicable, the inequalities of the other. No country can be in
the enjoyment of its full measure of prosperity without the presence
of a medium of exchange approximating to uniformity of value. What
is necessary as between the different nations of the earth is also important as between the inhabitants of different parts of the same country. With the first the precious metals constitute the chief medium of
circulation, and such also would be the case as to the last but for in-
ventions comparatively modern, which have furnished in place of gold
and silver a paper circulation. I do not propose to enter into a com-
parative analysis of the merits of the two systems. Such belonged
more properly to the period of the introduction of the paper system.
The speculative philosopher might find inducements to prosecute the
inquiry, but his researches could only lead him to conclude that the
paper system had probably better never have been introduced and
that society might have been much happier without it. The practical
statesman has a very different task to perform. He has to look at
things as they are, to take them as he finds them, to supply deficiencies
and to prune excesses as far as in him lies. The task of furnishing a
corrective for derangements of the paper medium with us is almost
inexpressibly great. The power exerted by the States to charter banking corporations, and which, having been carried to a great excess,
has filled the country with, in most of the States, an irredeemable
paper medium, is an evil which in some way or other requires a corrective. The rates at which bills of exchange are negotiated between
different parts of the country furnish an index of the value of the local
substitute for gold and silver, which is in many parts so far depreci-
ated as not to be received except at a large discount in payment of
debts or in the purchase of produce. It could earnestly be desired that
every bank not possessing the means of resumption should follow the
example of the late United States Bank of Pennsylvania and go into
liquidation rather than by refusing to do so to continue embarrassments in the way of solvent institutions, thereby augmenting the difficulties to the present condition of things. Whether this Government,
with due regard to the rights of the States, has any power to constrain

the banks either to resume specie payments or to force them into liquidation, is an inquiry which will not fail to claim your consideration. In view of the great advantages which are allowed the corporators, not among the least of which is the authority contained in most of their charters to make loans to three times the amount of their capital, thereby often deriving three times as much interest on the same amount of money as any individual is permitted by law to receive, no sufficient apology can be urged for a long-continued suspension of specie payments. Such suspension is productive of the greatest detriment to the public by expelling from circulation the precious metals and seriously hazarding the success of any effort that this Government can make to increase commercial facilities and to advance the public interests.

This is the more to be regretted and the indispensable necessity for a sound currency becomes the more manifest when we reflect on the vast amount of the internal commerce of the country. Of this we have no statistics nor just data for forming adequate opinions. But there can be no doubt but that the amount of transportation coastwise by sea, and the transportation inland by railroads and canals, and by steamboats and other modes of conveyance over the surface of our vast rivers and immense lakes, and the value of property carried and interchanged by these means form a general aggregate to which the foreign commerce of the country, large as it is, makes but a distant approach.

In the absence of any controlling power over this subject, which, by forcing a general resumption of specie payments, would at once have the effect of restoring a sound medium of exchange and would leave to the country but little to desire, what measure of relief falling within the limits of our constitutional competency does it become this Government to adopt? It was my painful duty at your last session, under the weight of most solemn obligations, to differ with Congress on the measures which it proposed for my approval, and which it doubtless regarded as corrective of existing evils. Subsequent reflection and events since occurring have only served to confirm me in the opinions then entertained and frankly expressed. I must be permitted to add that no scheme of governmental policy unaided by individual exertions can be available for ameliorating the present condition of things. Commercial modes of exchange and a good currency are but the necessary means of commerce and intercourse, not the direct productive sources of wealth. Wealth can only be accumulated by the earnings of industry and the savings of frugality, and nothing can be more ill judged than to look to facilities in borrowing or to a redundant circulation for the power of discharging pecuniary obligations. The country is full of resources and the people full of energy, and the great and permanent remedy for present embarrassments must be sought in industry, economy, the observance of good faith, and the favorable influence of time. In pursuance of a pledge given to

you in my last message to Congress, which pledge I urge as an
apology for adventuring to present you the details of any plan, the
Secretary of the Treasury will be ready to submit to you, should you
require it, a plan of finance which, while it throws around the public
treasure reasonable guards for its protection and rests on powers
acknowledged in practice to exist from the origin of the Government,
will at the same time furnish to the country a sound paper medium
and afford all reasonable facilities for regulating the exchanges. When
submitted, you will receive in it a plan amendatory of the existing
laws in relation to the Treasury Department, subordinate in all respects to the will of Congress directly and the will of the people
indirectly, self-sustaining should it be found in practice to realize
its promises in theory, and repealable at the pleasure of Congress. It
proposes by effectual restraints and by invoking the true spirit of our
institutions to separate the purse from the sword, or, more properly
to speak, denies any other control to the President over the agents
who may be selected to carry it into execution but what may be indispensably necessary to secure the fidelity of such agents, and by wise
regulations keeps plainly apart from each other private and public
funds. It contemplates the establishment of a board of control at the
seat of government, with agencies at prominent commercial points or
wherever else Congress shall direct, for the safe-keeping and disbursement of the public moneys, and a substitution at the option of the
public creditor of Treasury notes in lieu of gold and silver. It proposes
to limit the issues to an amount not to exceed $15,000,000 without the
express sanction of the legislative power. It also authorizes the receipt
of individual deposits of gold and silver to a limited amount, and the
granting certificates of deposit divided into such sums as may be
called for by the depositors. It proceeds a step further and authorizes the purchase and sale of domestic bills and drafts resting on a
real and substantial basis, payable at sight or having but a short
time to run, and drawn on places not less than 100 miles apart, which
authority, except in so far as may be necessary for Government purposes exclusively, is only to be exerted upon the express condition
that its exercise shall not be prohibited by the State in which the agency is situated. In order to cover the expenses incident to the plan,
it will be authorized to receive moderate premiums for certificates
issued on deposits and on bills bought and sold, and thus, as far as its
dealings extend, to furnish facilities to commercial intercourse at
the lowest possible rates and to subduct from the earnings of industry
the least possible sum. It uses the State banks at a distance from the
agencies as auxiliaries without imparting any power to trade in its
name. It is subjected to such guards and restraints as have appeared to
be necessary. It is the creature of law and exists only at the pleasure
of the Legislature. It is made to rest on an actual specie basis in
order to redeem the notes at the places of issue, produces no dangerous redundancy of circulation, affords no temptation to speculation, is
attended by no inflation of prices, is equable in its operation, makes

the Treasury notes (which it may use along with the certificates of deposit and the notes of specie-paying banks) convertible at the place where collected, receivable in payment of Government dues,and without violating any principle of the Constitution affords the Government and the people such facilities as are called for by the wants of both. Such, it has appeared to me, are its recommendations, and in view of them it will be submitted, whenever you may require it, to your consideration.

I am not able to perceive that any fair and candid objection can be urged against the plan, the principal outlines of which I have thus presented. I can not doubt but that the notes which it proposes to furnish at the voluntary option of the public creditor, issued in lieu of the revenue and its certificates of deposit, will be maintained at an equality with gold and silver everywhere. They are redeemable in gold and silver on demand at the places of issue. They are receivable everywhere in payment of Government dues. The Treasury notes are limited to an amount of one-fourth less than the estimated annual receipts of the Treasury, and in addition they rest upon the faith of the Government for their redemption. If all these assurances are not sufficient to make them available, then the idea, as it seems to me, of furnishing a sound paper medium of exchange may be entirely abandoned.

If a fear be indulged that the Government may be tempted to run into excess in its issues at any future day, it seems to me that no such apprehension can reasonably be entertained until all confidence in the representatives of the States and of the people, as well as of the people themselves, shall be lost. The weightiest considerations of policy require that the restraints now proposed to be thrown around the measure should not for light causes be removed. To argue against any proposed plan its liability to possible abuse is to reject every expedient, since everything dependent on human action is liable to abuse. Fifteen millions of Treasury notes may be issued as the maximum, but a discretionary power is to be given to the board of control under that sum, and every consideration will unite in leading them to feel their way with caution. For the first eight years of the existence of the late Bank of the United States its circulation barely exceeded $4,000,000, and for five of its most prosperous years it was about equal to $16,000,000; furthermore, the authority given to receive private deposits to a limited amount and to issue certificates in such sums as may be called for by the depositors may so far fill up the channels of circulation as greatly to diminish the necessity of any considerable issue of Treasury notes. A restraint upon the amount of private deposits has seemed to be indispensably necessary from an apprehension, thought to be well founded, that in any emergency of trade confidence might be so far shaken in the banks as to induce a withdrawal from them of private deposits with a view to insure their unquestionable safety when deposited with the Government, which might prove eminently disastrous to the State banks. Is it objected

that it is proposed to authorize the agencies to deal in bills of exchange? It is answered that such dealings are to be carried on at the
lowest possible premium, are made to rest on an unquestionably sound
basis, are designed to reimburse merely the expenses which would
otherwise devolve upon the Treasury, and are in strict subordination
to the decision of the Supreme Court in the case of the Bank of Augusta
against Earle, and other reported cases, and thereby avoids all conflict with State jurisdiction, which I hold to be indispensably requisite.
It leaves the banking privileges of the States without interference,
looks to the Treasury and the Union, and while furnishing every facility
to the first is careful of the interests of the last. But above all, it is
created by law, is amendable by law, and is repealable by law, and,
wedded as I am to no theory, but looking solely to the advancement of
the public good, I shall be among the very first to urge its repeal if it
be found not to subserve the purposes and objects for which it may be
created. Nor will the plan be submitted in any overweening confidence
in the sufficiency of my own judgment, but with much greater reliance on the wisdom and patriotism of Congress. I can not abandon this
subject without urging upon you in the most emphatic manner, whatever
may be your action on the suggestions which I have felt it to be my duty
to submit, to relieve the Chief Executive Magistrate, by any and all
constitutional means, from a controlling power over the public Treasury. If in the plan proposed should you deem it worthy of your consideration, that separation is not as complete as you may desire, you
will doubtless amend it in that particular. For myself, I disclaim all
desire to have any control over the public moneys other than what is
indispensably necessary to execute the laws which you may pass.

Nor can I fail to advert in this connection to the debts which many
of the States of the Union have contracted abroad and under which they
continue to labor. That indebtedness amounts to a sum not less than
$200,000,000 and which has been retributed to them for the most part
in works of internal improvement which are destined to prove of vast
importance in ultimately advancing their prosperity and wealth.
For the debts thus contracted the States are alone responsible. I can
do no more than express the belief that each State will feel itself
bound by every consideration of honor as well as of interest to meet
its engagements with punctuality. The failure, however, of any one
State to do so should in no degree affect the credit of the rest, and
the foreign capitalist will have no just cause to experience alarm as
to other State stocks because any one or more of the States may
neglect to provide with punctuality the means of redeeming their
engagements. Even such States, should there by any, considering the
great rapidity with which their resources are developing themselves,
will not fail to have to have the means at no very distant day to
redeem their obligations to the uttermost farthing; nor will I doubt
but that, in view of that honorable conduct which has evermore governed the States and the people of the Union, they will each and all resort

to every legitimate expedient before they will forego a faithful compliance with their obligations.

SECOND ANNUAL MESSAGE
December 6, 1842

While the Webster Ashburton Treaty had settled most outstanding issues between Britain and the United States during 1842, the issue of the slave trade continued to cause trouble. Tyler had expressed his opposition to the international slave trade and decried the idea that any ships might be using the American flag to conduct it. He denied the right of ships of any other nation, however, to detain or visit ships flying United States colors. In article eight of the Webster-Ashburton Treaty the United States had agreed to maintain a fleet of at least eighty guns on the coast of Africa to control such ships. This was not done and British actions continued to disturb Tyler.

The three major topics in his second annual message were foreign relations, tariff reform and the continued need for a constitutional banking institution. The sections dealing with the first two topics are included here. The third has been omitted because it was a restatement of the position taken in December, 1841.

We have continued reason to express our profound gratitude to the Great Creator of All Things for numberless benefits conferred upon us as a people. Blessed with genial seasons, the husbandman has his garners filled with abundance, and the necessaries of life, not to speak of its luxuries, abound in every direction. While in some other nations steady and industrious labor can hardly find the means of subsistence, the greatest evil which we have to encounter is a surplus of production beyond the home demand, which seeks, and with difficulty finds, a partial market in other regions. The health of the country, with partial exceptions, has for the past year been well preserved, and under their free and wise institutions the United States are rapidly advancing toward the consummation of the high destiny which an overruling Providence seems to have marked out for them. Exempt from domestic convulsion and at peace with all the world, we are left free to consult as to the best means of securing and advancing the happiness of the people. Such are the circumstances under which you now assemble in your respective chambers and which should lead us to unite in praise and thanksgiving to that great Being who made us and who preserves us as a nation.

I congratulate you, fellow-citizens, on the happy change in the aspect of our foreign affairs since my last annual message. Causes of complaint at that time existed between the United States and Great Britain which, attended by irritating circumstances, threatened most seriously the public peace. The difficulty of adjusting amicably the questions at issue between two countries was in no small degree augmented by the lapse of time since they had their origin. The opinions entertained by the Executive on several of the leading topics in dispute were frankly set forth in the message at the opening of your late session. The appointment of a special minister by Great Britain to the United States with power to negotiate upon most of the points of difference indicated a desire on her part amicably to adjust them, and that minister was met by the Executive in the same spirit which had dictated his mission. The treaty consequent thereon having been duly ratified by the two Governments, a copy, together with the correspondence which accompanied it, is herewith communicated. I trust that whilst you may see in it nothing objectionable, it may be the means of preserving for an indefinite period the amicable relations happily existing between the two Governments. The question of peace or war between the United States and Great Britain is a question of the deepest interest, not only to themselves, but to the civilized world, since it is scarcely possible that a war could exist between them without endangering the peace of Christendom. The immediate effect of the treaty upon ourselves will be felt in the security afforded to mercantile enterprise, which, no longer apprehensive of interruption, adventures its speculations in the most distant seas, and, freighted with the diversified productions of every land, returns to bless our own. There is nothing in the treaty which in the slightest degree compromits the honor or dignity of either nation. Next to the settlement of the boundary line, which must always be a matter of difficulty between states as between individuals, the question which seemed to threaten the greatest embarrassment was that connected with the African slave trade.

By the tenth article of the treaty of Ghent it was expressly declared that —

> Whereas the traffic in slaves is irreconcilable with the principles of humanity and justice, and whereas both His Majesty and the United States are desirous of continuing their efforts to promote its entire abolition, it is hereby agreed that both the contracting parties shall use their best endeavors to accomplish so desirable an object.

In the enforcement of the laws and treaty stipulations of Great Britain a practice had threatened to grow up on the part of its cruisers of subjecting to visitation ships sailing under the American flag, which, while it seriously involved our maritime rights, would subject to vexation a branch of our trade which was daily increasing, and which required the fostering care of Government. And although Lord Aberdeen in his correspondence with the American envoys at London expressly disclaimed all right to detain an American ship on the high seas, even if found with a cargo of slaves on board, and restricted the British pretension to a mere claim to visit and inquire, yet it could not well be discerned by the Executive of the United States how such visit and inquiry would be made without detention on the voyage and consequent interruption to the trade. It was regarded as the right of search presented only in a new form and expressed in different words, and I therefore felt it to be my duty distinctly to declare in my annual message to Congress that no such concession could be made, and that the United States had both the will and the ability to enforce their own laws and to protect their flag from being used for purposes wholly forbidden by those laws and abnoxious to the moral censure of the world. Taking the message as his letter of instructions, our then minister at Paris felt himself required to assume the same ground in a remonstrance which he felt it to be his duty to present to Mr. Guizot, and through him to the King of the French, against what has been called the "quintuple treaty;" and his conduct in this respect met with the approval of this Government. In close conformity with these views the eighth article of the treaty was framed, which provides "that each nation shall keep afloat in the African seas a force not less than 80 guns, to act separately and apart, under instructions from their respective Governments, and for the enforcement of their respective laws and obligations." From this it will be seen that the ground assumed in the message has been fully maintained at the same time that the stipulations of the treaty of Ghent are to carried out in good faith by the two countries, and that all pretense is removed for interference with our commerce for any purpose whatever by a foreign government. While, therefore, the United States have been standing up for the freedom of the seas, they have not thought proper to make that a pretext for avoiding a fulfillment of their treaty stipulations or a ground for giving countenance to a trade reprobated by our laws. A similar arrangement by the other great powers could not fail to sweep from the ocean the slave trade without the interpolation of any new principle into the maritime code. We may be permitted to hope that the example thus set will be followed by some if not all of them. We thereby also afford suitable protection to the fair trader in those seas, thus fulfilling at the same time the dictates of a sound policy and complying with the claims of justice and humanity.

It would have furnished additional cause for congratulation if the treaty could have embraced all subjects calculated in future to lead to a misunderstanding between the two Governments. The Territory of the United States commonly called the Oregon Territory, lying on the Pacific Ocean north of the forty-second degree of latitude, to a portion of which Great Britain lays claim, begins to attract the attention of our fellow-citizens, and the tide of population which has re-claimed what was so lately an unbroken wilderness in more contiguous regions is preparing to flow over those vast districts which stretch from the Rocky Mountains to the Pacific Ocean. In advance of the acquirement of individual rights to these lands, sound policy dictates that every effort should be resorted to by the two Governments to settle their respective claims. It became manifest at an early hour of the late negotiations that any attempt for the time being satisfactorily to determine those rights would lead to a protracted discussion, which might embrace in its failure other more pressing matters, and the Executive did not regard it as proper to waive all the advantages of an honorable adjustment of other difficulties of great magnitude and importance because this, not so immediately pressing, stood in the way. Although the difficulty referred to may not for several years to come involve the peace of the two countries, yet I shall not delay to urge on Great Britain the importance of its early settlement. Nor will other matters of commercial importance to the two countries be overlooked and I have good reason to believe that it will comport with the policy of England, as it does with that of the United States, to seize upon this moment, when most of the causes of irritation have passed away, to cement the peace and amity of the two countries by wisely removing all grounds of probable future collison.

With the other powers of Europe our relations continue on the most amicable footing. Treaties now existing with them should be rigidly pbserved, and every opportunity compatible with the interests of the United States should be seized upon to enlarge the basis of commercial intercourse. Peace with all the world is the true foundation of our policy, which can only be rendered permanent by the practice of equal and impartial justice to all. Our great desire should be to enter only into that rivalry which looks to the general good in the cultivation of the sciences, the enlargement of the field for the exercise of the mechanical arts, and the spread of commerce – that great civilizer – to every land and sea. Carefully abstaining from interference in all questions exclusively referring themselves to the political interest of Europe, we may be permitted to hope an equal exemption from the interference of European Governments in what relates to the States of the American continent.

On the 23d of April last the commissioners on the part of the United States under the convention with the Mexican Republic of the 11th of April, 1839, made to the proper Department a final report in relation to the proceedings of the commission. From this it appears that the total amount awarded to the claimants by the commissioners and the umpire appointed under that convention was $2,026,079.68. The arbiter having considered that his functions were required by the convention to terminate at the same time with those of the commissioners, returned to the board, undecided for want of time, claims which had been allowed by the American commissioners to the amount of

$928,620.88. Other claims, in which the amount sought to be recovered was $3,336,837.05, were submitted to the board too late for its consideration. The minister of the United States at Mexico has been duly authorized to make demand for payment of the awards according to the terms of the convention and the provisions of the act of Congress of the 12th of June, 1840. He has also been instructed to communicate to that Government the expectations of the Government of the United States in relation to those claims which were not disposed of according to the provisions of the convention, and all others of citizens of the United States against the Mexican Government. He has also been furnished with other instructions, to be followed by him in case the Government of Mexico should not find itself in a condition to make present payment of the amount of the awards in specie or its equivalent.

I am happy to be able to say that information which is esteemed favorable both to a just satisfaction of the awards and a reasonable provision for other claims has been recently received from Mr. Thompson, the minister of the United States, who has promptly and efficiently executed the instructions of his Government in regard to this important subject.

The citizens of the United States who accompanied the late Texan expedition to Santa Fe, and who were wrongfully taken and held as prisoners of war in Mexico, have all been liberated.

A correspondence has taken place between the Department of State and the Mexican minister of foreign affairs upon the complaint of Mexico that citizens of the United States were permitted to give aid to the inhabitants of Texas in the war existing between her and that Republic. Copies of this correspondence are herewith communicated to Congress, together with copies of letters on the same subject addressed to the diplomatic corps at Mexico by the American minister and the Mexican secretary of state.

Mexico has though proper to reciprocate the mission of the United States to that Government by accrediting to this a minister of the same rank as that of the representative of the United States in Mexico. From the circumstances connected with his mission favorable results are anticipated from it. It is so obviously for the interest of both countries as neighbors and friends that all just causes of mutual dissatisfaction should be removed that it is to be hoped neither will omit or delay the employment of any practicable and honorable means to accomplish that end.

*   *   *   *

The balance in the Treasury on the 1st of January, 1842, exclusive of the amount deposited with the States, trust funds, and indemnities, was $230,483.68. The receipts into the Treasury during the three quarters of the present year from all sources amount to $26,616,593.78,

of which more than fourteen millions were received from customs and
about one million from the public lands. The receipts for the fourth
quarter are estimated at nearly eight millions, of which four millions
are expected from customs and three millions and a half from loans
and Treasury notes. The expenditures of the first three quarters of
the present year exceed twenty-six millions, and those estimated for
the fourth quarter amount to about eight millions; and it is anticipated
there will be a deficiency of half a million on the 1st of January next,
but that the amount of outstanding warrants (estimated at $800,000)
will leave an actual balance of about $224,000 in the Treasury.
Among the expenditures of this year are more than eight millions for
the public debt and about $600,000 on account of the distribtuion to
the States of the proceeds of sales of the public lands.

The present tariff of duties was somewhat hastily and hurriedly
passed near the close of the late session of Congress. That it should
have defects can therefore be surprising to no one. To remedy such
defects as may be found to exist in any of its numerous provisions
will not fail to claim your seious attention. It may well merit inquiry
whether the exaction of all duties in cash does not call for the intro-
ductions of a system which has proved highly beneficial in countries
where it has been adopted. I refer to the warehousing system. The
first and most prominent effect which it would produce would be to
protect the market alike against redundant or deficient supplies of
foreign fabrics, both of which in the long run are injurious as well to
the manufacturer as the importer The quantity of goods in store being
at all times readily known, it would enable the importer with an approach to accuracy to ascertain the actual wants of the market and to
regulate himself accordingly. If, however, he should fall into error by
importing an excess above the public wants, he could readily correct
its evils by availing himself of the benefits and advantages of the
system thus established. In the storehouse the goods imported would
await the demand of the market and their issues would be governed by
the fixed principles of demand and supply. Thus an approximation
would be made to a steadiness and uniformity of price, which if attainable would conduce to the decided advantage of mercantile and mechanical operations.

The apprehension may be well entertained that without something
to ameliorate the rigor of cash payments the entire import trade may
fall into the hands of a few wealthy capitalists in this country and in
Europe. The small importer, who requires all the money he can raise
for investments abroad and who can but ill afford to pay the lowest
duty, would have to subduct in advance a portion of his funds in order
to pay the duties, and would lose the interest upon the amount thus
paid for all the time the goods might remain unsold, which might
absorb his profits. The rich capitalist, abroad as well as at home,
would thus possess after a short time an almost exclusive monopoly
of the import trade, and laws designed for the benefit of all would

thus operate for the benefit of a few — a result wholly uncongenial with the spirit of our institutions and antirepublican in all its tendencies. The warehousing system would enable the importer to watch the market and to select his own time for offering his goods for sale. A profitable portion of the carrying trade in articles entered for the benefit of drawback must also be most seriously affected without the adoption of some expedient to relieve the cash system. The warehousing system would afford that relief since the carrier would have a safe recourse to the public storehouses and might without advancing the duty reship within some reasonable period to foreign ports. A further effect of the measure would be to supersede the system of drawbacks, thereby effectually protecting the Government against fraud, as the right of debenture would not attach to goods after their withdrawal from the public stores.

In revising the existing tariff of duties, should you deem it proper to do so at your present session, I can only repeat the suggestions and recommendations which upon several occasions I have heretofore felt it to be my duty to offer to Congress. The great primary and controlling interest of the American people is union- union not only in the mere forms of government, forms which may be broken, but union founded in an attachment of States and individuals for each other. This union in sentiment and feeling can only be preserved by the adoption of that course of policy which, neither giving exclusive benefits to some nor imposing unnecessary burthens upon others, shall consult the interests of all by pursuing a course of moderation and thereby seeking to harmonnize public opinion, and causing the people everywhere to feel and to know that the Government is careful of the interests of all alike. Nor is there any subject in regard to which moderation, connected with a wise discrimination, is more necessary than in the imposition of duties on imports. Whether reference be had to revenue, the primary object in the imposition of taxes, or to the incidents which necessarily flow from their imposition, this is entirely true. Extravagant duties defeat their end and object, not only by exciting in the public mind an hostility to the manufacturing interests, but by inducing a system of smuggling on an extensive scale and the practice of every manner of fraud upon the revenue, which the utmost vigilance of Government can not effectually supress. An opposite course of policy would be attended by results essentially different, of which every interest of society, and none more than those of the manufacturer, would reap important advantages. Among the most striking of its benefits would be that derived from the general acquiescence of the country in its support and the consequent permanency and stability which would be given to all the operations of industry. It can not be too often repeated that no system of legislation can be wise which is fluctuating and uncertain. No interest can thrive under it. The prudent capitalist will never adventure his capital in manufacturing establishments, or in any other leading pursuit of life, if there exists a state of uncertainty as

to whether the Government will repeal to-morrow what it has enacted
to-day. Fitful profits, however high, if threatened with a ruinous reduction by a vacillating policy on the part of Government, will scarcely
tempt him to trust the money which he has acquired by a life of labor
upon the uncertain adventure. I therefore, in the spirit of conciliation,
and influenced by no other disire than to rescue the great interests
of the country from the vortex of political contention, and in the discharge of the high and solemn duties of the place which I now occupy,
recommend moderate duties, imposed with a wise discrimination as
to their several objects, as being not only most likely to be durable,
but most advantageous to every interest of society.

THIRD ANNUAL MESSAGE

December 5, 1843

*Foreign relations, the tariff and banking reform continued
to be the major topics of Tyler's annual messages. His
arguments on the latter two subjects remained essentially
the same but had less force because, even without the
measures advocated by Tyler, the economy of the United
States seemed to be booming and the government was no
longer running a deficit. Oregon and Texas had become
the major issues of foreign policy and the portions of the
annual message of 1843 that considered those areas are
reproduced below.*

Since the last adjournment of Congress the Executive has relaxed
no effort to render indestructible the relations of amity which so
happily exist between the United States and other countries. The treaty
lately concluded with Great Britain has tended greatly to increase the
good understanding which a reciprocity of interests is calculated to
encourage, and it is most ardently to be hoped that nothing may trans-
pire to interrupt the relations of amity which it is so obviously the
policy of both nations to cultivate. A question of much importance still
remains to be adjusted between them. The territorial limits of the
two countries in relation to what is commonly known as the Oregon
Territory still remain in dispute. The United States would be at all
times indisposed to aggrandize itself at the expense of any other nation;
but while they would be restrained by principles of honor, which should
govern the conduct of nations as well as that of individuals, from set-

ting up a demand for territory which does not belong to them, they would as unwillingly consent to a surrender of their rights. After the most rigid and, as far as practicable, unbiased examination of the subject, the United States have always contended that their rights appertain to the entire region of country lying on the Pacific and embraced with 42° and 54° 40' of north latitude. This claim being controverted by Great Britain, those who have preceded the present Executive — actuated, no doubt, by an earnest desire to adjust the matter upon terms mutually satisfactory to both countries — have caused to be submitted to the British Government propositions for settlement and final adjustment, which, however, have not proved heretofore acceptable to it. Our minister at London has, under instructions, again brought the subject to the consideration of that Government, and while nothing will be done to compromit the rights or honor of the United States, every proper expedient will be resorted to in order to bring the negotiation now in the progress of resumption to a speedy and happy termination. In the meantime, it is proper to remark that many of our citizens are either already established in the Territory or are on their way thither for the purpose of forming permanent settlements, while others are preparing to follow; and in view of these facts I must repeat the recommendation contained in previous messages for the establishment contained in previous messages for the establishment of military posts at such places on the line of travel as well furnish security and protection to our hardy adventurers against hostile tribes of Indians inhabiting those extensive regions. Our laws should also follow them, so modified as the circumstances of the case may seem to require. Under the influence of our free system of government many republics are destined to spring up at no distant day on the shores of the Pacific similar in policy and in feeling to those existing on this side of the Rocky Mountains, and giving a wider and more extensive spread to the principles of civil and religious liberty.

*   *   *   *   *

I communicate herewith certain dispatches received from our minister at Mexico, and also a correspondence which has recently occurred between the envoy from that Republic and the Secretary of State. It must but be regarded as not a little extraordinary that the Government of Mexico, in anticipation of a public discussion (which it has been pleased to infer from newspaper publications as likely to take place in Congress, relating to the annexation of Texas to the United States), should have so far anticipated the result of such discussion as to have announced its determination to visit any such anticipated decision by a formal declaration of war against the United States. If designed to prevent Congress from introducing that question as a fit subject for its calm deliberate and final judgment, the Executive has no reason to doubt that it will entirely fail of its object. The representatives of a brave and patriotic people will suffer no apprehension of future consequences to embarrass them in the course of their proposed deliberations, nor will the executive department of the Government fail for any such cause to discharge its whole duty to the country.

The war which has existed for so long a time between Mexico and Texas has since the battle of San Jacinto consisted for the most part of predatory incursions, which, while they have been attended with much of suffering to individuals and have kept the borders of the two countries in a state of constant alarm, have failed to approach to any definitive result. Mexico has fitted out no formidable armament by land or by sea for the subjugation of Texas. Eight years have now elapsed since Texas declared her independence of Mexico, and during that time she has been recognized as a sovereign power by several of the principal civilized states. Mexico, nevertheless, perseveres in her plans of reconquest, and refuses to recognize her independence. The predatory incursions to which I have alluded have been attended in one instance with the breaking up of the courts of justice, by the seizing upon the persons of the judges, jury, and officers of the court and dragging them along with unarmed, and therefore noncombatant, citizens into a cruel and oppressive bondage, thus leaving crime to go unpunished and immorality to pass unreproved. A border warfare is evermore to be deprecated, and over such a war as has existed for so many years between these two States humanity has had great cause to lament. Nor is such a condition of things to be deplored only because of the individual suffering attendant upon it. The effects are far more extensive. The Creator of the Universe has given man the earth for his resting place and its fruits for this subsistence. Whatever, therefore, shall make the first or any part of it a scene of desolation affects injuriously his heritage and may be regarded as a general calamity. Wars may sometimes be necessary, but all nations have a common interest in bringing them speedily to a close. The United States have an immediate interest in seeing an end put to the state of hostilities existing between Mexico and Texas. They are our neighbors, of the same continent, with whom we are not only desirous of cultivating the relations of amity, but of the most extended commercial intercourse, and to practice all the rites of a neighborhood hospitality. Our own interests are involved in the matter, since, however neutral may be our course of policy, we can not hope to escape the effects of a spirit of jealousy on the part of both of the powers. Nor can this Government be indifferent to the fact that a warfare such as is waged between those two nations is calculated to weaken both powers and finally to render them – and especially the weaker of the two – the subjects of interference on the part of stronger and more powerful nations, who, intent only on advancing their own peculiar views, may sooner or later attempt to bring about a compliance with terms as the condition of their interposition alike derogatory to the nation granting them and deterimental to the interests of the United States. We could not be expected quietly to permit any such interference to our disadvantage. Considering that Texas is separated from the United States by a mere geographical line; that her territory, in the opinion of many, down to a late period formed a portion of the territory of the United States; that it is homogeneous in its population and pursuits with the adjoining States, makes contributions to the commerce of the world in the same articles with them, and that most of her inhabitants have been citizens of the United States, speak the same language, and live under similar political institutions with ourselves, this Government is bound by every consideration of interest as well as of sympathy to see that she shall be left free to act, especially in regard to her domestic affairs, unawed by force and unrestrained by the policy or views of other countries. In full view of all these considerations, the Executive has not hesitated to express to the Government of Mexico how deeply it deprecated a continuance of the war and how anxiously it desired to witness its termination. I can not but think that it becomes the United States, as the oldest of the American Republics, to hold a language to Mexico upon this subject of an unambiguous character, It is time that this war had ceased. There must be a limit to all wars, and if the parent state after an eight years' struggle has failed to reduce to submission a portion of its subjects standing out in revolt against it, and who have not only proclaimed themselves to be independent, but have been recognized as such by other powers, she ought not to expect that other nations will quietly look on, to their obvious injury, upon a protraction of hostilities. These United States threw off their colonial dependence and established independent governments, and Great Britain, after having wasted her energies in the attempt to subdue them for a less period than Mexico has attempted to subjugate Texas, had the wisdom and justice to acknowledge their independence thereby recognizing the obligation which rested on her as one of the family of nations. An example thus set by one of the proudest as well as most powerful nations of the earth it could in no way disparage Mexico to imitate. While, therefore, the Executive would deplore any collision with Mexico or any disturbance of the friendly relations which exist between the two countries, it can not permit that Government to control its policy, whatever it may be, toward Texas, but will treat her — as by the recognition of her independence the United States have long since declared they would do — as entirely independent of Mexico. The high obligations of public duty may enforce from the constituted authorities of the United States a policy which the course persevered in by Mexico will have mainly contributed to produce and the Executive in such a contingency will with confidence throw itself upon the patriotism of the people to sustain the Government in its course of action.

Measures of an unusual character have recently been adopted by the Mexican Government, calculated in no small degree to affect the trade of other nations with Mexico and to operate injuriously to the United States. All foreigners, by a decree of the 23rd day of September and after six months from the day of its promulgation, are forbidden to carry on the business of selling by retail any goods within the confines of Mexico. Against this decree our minister has not failed to remonstrate.

The trade heretofore carried on by our citizens with Santa Fe, in which much capital was already invested and which was becoming of daily increasing importance, has suddenly been arrested by a decree of virtual prohibition on the part of the Mexican Government. Whatever may be the right of Mexico to prohibit any particular course of trade to the citizens or subjects of foreign powers, this late procedure, to say the least of it wears a harsh and unfriendly aspect.

The installments on the claims recently settled by the convention with Mexico have been punctually paid as they have fallen due, and our minister is engaged in urging the establishment of a new commission in pursuance of the convention for the settlement of unadjusted claims.

*   *   *   *

JOHN TYLER

SUBMISSION OF TREATY WITH TEXAS

April 22, 1844

*After failing to obtain the type of banking and fiscal re-
form desired and being repudiated by the Whig party leaders, Tyler came to place more and more emphasis on the
annexation of Texas as the chief task to be accomplished
by his administration. In April, 1844, he submitted the
treaty of annexation to the Senate. In his accompanying
message he expressed his position on the legality of the
annexation, the advantages to the United States of the
annexation and the dangers that might develop if the opportunity were not accepted. He recognized two arguments
against the treaty, possible hostility on the part of Mexico
and the idea that the United States would become too
large to govern under republican institutions, but dis-
counted both. While he stressed the similarity of Texas
to the nearby areas of the United States, he did not men-
tion the controversy over the expansion of slaveholding
territory.*

Washington, April 22, 1844

To the Senate of the United States:

I transmit herewith, for your approval and ratification, a treaty
which I have caused to be negotiated between the United States and
Texas, whereby the latter on the conditions therein set forth, has
transferred and conveyed all its right of separate and independent
sovereignty and jurisdiction to the United States. In taking so important a step I have been influenced by what appeared to me to be the
most controlling considerations of public policy and the general good,
and in having accomplished it, should it meet with your approval, the
Government will have succeeded in reclaiming a territory which
formerly constituted a portion, as it is confidently believed, of its
domain under the treaty of cession of 1803 by France to the United
States.

The country thus proposed to be annexed has been settled principally
by persons from the United States, who emigrated on the invitation of
both Spain and Mexico, and who carried with them into the wilderness
which they have partially reclaimed the laws, customs, and political
and domestic institutions of their native land. They are deeply in-
doctrinated in all the principles of civil liberty, and will bring along
with them in the act of reassociation devotion to our Union and a firm
and inflexible resolution to assist in maintaining the public liberty
unimpaired − a consideration which, as it appears to me, is to be

regarded as of no small moment. The country itself thus obtained is
of incalculable value in an agricultural and commercial point of view.
To a soil of inexhaustible fertility it unites a genial and healthy climate, and is destined at a day not distant to make large contributions
to the commerce of the world. Its territory is separated from the
United States in part by an imaginary line, and by the river Sabine for
a distance of 310 miles, and its productions are the same with those of
many of the contiguous States of the Union. Such is the country, such
are its inhabitants, and such its capacities to add to the general wealth
of the Union. As to the latter, it may be safely asserted that in the
magnitude of its productions it will equal in a short time, under the
protecting care of this Government, if it does not surpass, the com-
bined production of many of the States of the Confederacy. A new and
powerful impulse will thus be given to the navigating interest of the
country, which will be chiefly engrossed by our fellow-citizens of
the Eastern and Middle States, who have already attained a remark-
able degree of prosperity by the partial monopoly they have enjoyed
of the carrying trade of the Union, particularly the coastwise trade,
which this new acquisition is destined in time, and that not distant,
to swell to a magnitude which can not easily be computed, while the
addition made to the boundaries of the home market thus secured to
their mining, manufacturing, and mechanical skill and industry will be
of a character the most commanding and important. Such are some of
the many advantages which will accrue to the Eastern and Middle
States by the ratification of the treaty —advantages the extent of which
it is impossible to estimate with accuracy or properly to appreciate.
Texas, being adapted to the culture of cotton, sugar, and rice, and
devoting most of her energies to the rising of these productions, will
open an extensive market to the Western States in the important articles
of beef, pork, horses, mules, etc., as well as in breadstuffs. At the
same time, the Sourthern and South eastern States will find in the fact
of annexation protection and security to their peace and tranquility,
as well against all domestic as foreign efforts to disturb them, thus
consecrating anew the union of the States and holding out the promise
of its perpetual duration. Thus at the same time that the tide of public
prosperity is greatly swollen, an appeal of what appears to the Executive to be of an imposing, if not of a resistless, character is made to
the interests of every portion of the country. Agriculture, which would
have a new and extensive market opened for its produce; commerce,
whose ships would be freighted with the rich productions of an extensive and fertile region; and the mechanical arts, in all their various
ramifications, would seem to unite in one universal demand for the
ratification of the treaty. But important as these considerations may
appear, they are to be regarded as but secondary to others. Texas, for
reasons deemed sufficient by herself, threw off her dependence on
Mexico as far back as 1836, and consummated her independence by
the battle of San Jacinto in the same year, since which period Mexico
has attempted no serious invasion of her territory, but the contest has

assumed features of a mere border war, characterized by acts revolting to humanity. In the year 1836 Texas adopted her constitution, under which she has existed as a soverign power ever since, having been recognized as such by many of the principal powers of the world; and contemporaneously with its adoption, by a solemn vote of her people, embracing all her population but ninety-three persons, declared her anxious desire to be admitted into association with the United States as a portion of their territory. This vote, thus solemnly taken, has never been reversed, and now by the action of her constituted authorities, sustained as it is by popular sentiment, she reaffirms her desire for annexation. This course has been adopted by her without the employment of any sinister measures on the part of this Government. No intrigue has been set on foot to accomplish it. Texas herself wills it, and the Executive of the United States, concurring with her, has seen no sufficient reason to avoid the consummation of an act esteemed to be so desirable by both. It can not be denied that Texas is greatly depressed in her energies by her long-protracted war with Mexico. Under these circumstances it is but natural that she should seek for safety and repose under the protection of some stronger power, and it is equally so that her people should turn to the United States, the land of their birth, in the first instance in the pursuit of such protection. She has often before made known her wishes, but her advances have to this time been repelled. The Executive of the United States sees no longer any cause for pursuing such a course. The hazard of now defeating her wishes may be of the most fatal tendency. It might lead, and most probably would to such an entire alienation of sentiment and feeling as would inevitably induce her to look elsewhere for aid, and force her either to enter into dangerous alliances with other nations, who, looking with more wisdom to their own interests, would, it is fairly to be presumed, readily adopt such expedients; or she would hold out the proffer of discriminating duties in trade and commerce in order to secure the necessary assistance. Whatever step she might adopt looking to this object would prove disastrous in the highest degree to the interests of the whole Union. To say nothing of the impolicy of our permitting the carrying trade and home market of such a country to pass out of our hands into those of a commercial rival, the Government, in the first place, would be certain to suffer most disastrously in its revenue by the introduction of a system of smuggling upon an extensive scale, which an army of custom-house officers could not prevent, and which would operate to affect injuriously the interests of all the industrial classes of this country. Hence would arise constant collisions between the inhabitants of the two countries, which would evermore endanger their peace. A large increase of the military force of the United States would inevitably follow, thus devolving upon the people new and extraordinary burdens in order not only to protect them from the danger of daily collision with Texas herself, but to guard their border inhabitants against hostile inroads, so easily excited on the part of the numerous and warlike tribes of Indians

dwelling in their neighborhood. Texas would undoubtedly be unable
for many years to come, if at any time, to resist unaided and alone
the military power of the United States; but it is not extravagant to
suppose that nations reaping a rich harvest from her trade, secured
to them by advantageous treaties, would be induced to take part with
her in any conflict with us, from the strongest considerations of
public policy. Such a state of things might subject to devastation the
territory of contiguous States, and would cost the country in a single
campaign more treasure, thrice told over, than is stipulated to be
paid and reimbursed by the treaty now proposed for ratification. I
will not permit myself to dwell on this view of the subject. Consequences of a fatal character to the peace of the Union, and even to
the preservation of the Union itself, might be dwelt upon. They will
not, however, fail to occur to the mind of the Senate and of the country.
Nor do I indulge in any vague conjectures of the future. The documents
now transmitted along with the treaty lead to the conclusion, as inevitable, that if the boon now tendered be rejected Texas will seek for
the friendship of others. In contemplating such a contingency it can not
be overlooked that the United States are already almost surrounded
by the possessions of European powers. The Canadas, New Brunswick, and Nova Scotia, the islands in the American seas, with Texas
trammeled by treaties of alliance or of a commercial character dif-
fering in policy from that of the United States, would complete the
circle. Texas voluntarily steps forth, upon terms of perfect honor and
good faith to all nations, to ask to be annexed to the Union. As an independent sovereignty her right to do this is unquestionable. In doing
so she gives no cause of umbrage to any other powers; her people desire it, and there is no slavish transfer of her sovereignty and independence. She has for eight years maintained her independence against all
efforts to subdue her. She has been recognized as independent by many
of the most prominent of the family of nations, and that recognition,
so far as they are concerned, places her in a position, without giving
any just cause of umbrage to them, to surrender her sovereignty at
her own will and pleasure. The United States, actuated evermore by
a spirit of justice, has desired by the stipulations of the treaty to
render justice to all. They have made provision for the payment of the
public debt of Texas. We look to her ample and fertile domain as the
certain means of accomplishing this; but this is a matter between the
United States and Texas, and, with which other Governments have
nothing to do. Our right to receive the rich grant tendered by Texas is
perfect, and this Government should not, having due respect either to
its own honor or its own interests, permit its course of policy to be
interrupted by the interference of other powers, even if such interference were threatened. The question is one purely American. In the
acquisition, while we abstain most carefully from all that could interrupt the public peace, we claim the right to exercise a due regard to
our own. This Government can not consistently with its honor permit
any such interference. With equal, if not greater, propriety might the

United States demand of other governments to surrender their numerous and valuable acquisitions made in past time at numberless places
on the surface of the globe, whereby they have added to their power
and enlarged their resources.

To Mexico the Executive is disposed to pursue a course concilia-
tory in its character and at the same time to render her the most
ample justice by conventions and stipulations not inconsistent with the
rights and dignity of the Government. It is actuated by no spirit of
unjust aggrandizement, but looks only to its own security. It has
made known to Mexico at several periods its extreme anxiety to witness the termination of hostilities between that country and Texas.
Its wishes, however, have been entirely disregarded. It has ever been
ready to urge an adjustment of the dispute upon terms mutually advantageous to both. It will be ready at all times to hear and discuss
any claims Mexico may think she has on the justice of the United
States and to adjust any that may be deemed to be so on the most liberal terms. There is no desire on the part of the Executive to wound
her pride or affect injuriously her interest, but at the same time it
can not compromit by any delay in its action the essential interests of
the United States. Mexico has no right to ask or expect this of us; we
deal rightfully withTexas as an independent power. The war which has
been waged for eight years has resulted only in the conviction with all
others than herself that Texas can not be reconquered. I can not but
repeat the opinion expressed in my message at the opening of Congress
that it is time it had ceased. The Executive, while it could not look
upon its longer continuance without the greatest uneasiness, has,
nevertheless, for all past time preserved a course of strict neutrality.
It could not be ignorant of the fact of the exhaustion which a war of so
long a duration had produced. Least of all was it ignorant of the anxiety of other powers to induce Mexico to enter into terms of recon-
ciliation with Texas, which, affecting the domestic institutions of Texas,
would operate most injuriously upon the United States and might most
seriously threaten the existence of this happy Union. Nor could it be
unacquainted with the fact that although foreign governments might
disavow all design to disturb the relations which exist under the Constitution between these States, yet that one, the most powerful amongst
them, had not failed to declare its marked and decided hostility to
the chief feature in those relations and its purpose on all suitable occasions to urge upon Mexico the adoption of such a course in negotiating with Texas as to produce the obliteration of that feature from her
domestic policy as one of the conditions of her recognition by Mexico
as an independent state. The Executive was also aware of the fact that
formidable associations of persons, the subjects of foreign powers,
existed, who were directing their utmost efforts to the accomplishment
of this object. To these conclusions it was inevitably brought by the
documents now submitted to the Senate. I repeat, the Executive saw
Texas in a state of almost hopeless exhaustion, and the question was

narrowed down to the simple proposition whether the United States should accept the boon of annexation upon fair and even liberal terms, or, by refusing to do so, force Texas to seek refuge in the arms of some other power, either through a treaty of alliance, offensive and defensive, or the adoption of some other expedient which might virtually make her tributary to such power and dependent upon it for all future time. The Executive has full reason to believe that such would have been the result without its interposition, and that such will be the result in the event either of unnecessary delay in the ratification or of the rejection of the proposed treaty.

In full view, then, of the highest public duty, and as a measure of security against evils incalculably great, the Executive has entered into the negotiation, the fruits of which are now submitted to the Senate. Independent of the urgent reasons which existed for the step it has taken, it might safely invoke the fact (which it confidently believes) that there exists no civilized government on earth having a voluntary tender made it of a domain so rich and fertile, so replete with all that can add to national greatness and wealth, and so necessary to its peace and safety that would reject the offer. Nor are other powers, Mexico inclusive, likely in any degree to be injuriously affected by the ratification of the treaty. The prosperity of Texas will be equally interesting to all; in the increase of the general commerce of the world that prosperity will be secured by annexation.

But one view of the subject remains to be presented. It grows out of the proposed enlargement of our territory. From this, I am free to confess, I see no danger. The federative system is susceptible of the greatest extension compatible with the ability of the representation of the most distant State or Territory to reach the seat of Government in time to participate in the functions of legislation and to make known the wants of the constituent body. Our confederated Republic consisted originally of thirteen members. It now consists of twice that number, while applications are before Congress to permit other additions. This addition of new States has served to strengthen rather than to weaken the Union. New interests have sprung up, which require the united power of all, through the action of the common Government, to protect and defend upon the high seas and in foreign parts. Each State commits with perfect security to that common Government those great interests growing out of our relations with other nations of the world, and which equally involve the good of all the States. Its domestic concerns are left to its own exclusive management. But if there were any force in the objection it would seem to require an immediate abandonment of territorial possessions which lie in the distance and stretch to a faroff sea, and yet no one would be found, it is believed, ready to recommend such an abandonment. Texas lies at our very doors and in our immediate vicinity.

Under every view which I have been able to take of the subject, I think that the interests of our common constituents, the people of all the States, and a love of the Union left the Executive no other alternative than to negotiate the treaty. The high and solemn duty of ratifying or rejecting it is wisely devolved on the Senate by the Constitution of the United States.

JOHN TYLER

MESSAGES REGARDING MEXICO AND TEXAS
May 15, 1844

Tyler submitted two reports to the Senate May 15, 1844, in response to enquiries from that body concerning steps that were or were not being taken considering the possibility of a declaration of War by Mexico if the United States annexed Texas.

In answer to the resolution of the Senate of the 13th instant, requesting to be informed 'whether, since the commencement of the negotiations which resulted in the treaty now before the Senate for the annexation of Texas to the United States, any military preparation has been made or ordered by the President for or in anticipation of war, and, if so, for what cause, and with whom was such war apprehended, and what are the preparations that have been made or ordered; has any movement or assemblage or disposition of any of the military or naval forces of the United States been made or ordered with a view to such hostilities; and to communicate to the Senate copies of all orders or directions given for any such preparation or for any such movement or disposition or for the future conduct of such military or naval forces, "I have to inform the Senate that, in consequence of the declaration of Mexico communicated to this Government and by me laid before Congress at the opening of its present session, announcing the determination of Mexico to regard as a declaration of war against her by the United States the definitive ratification of any treaty with Texas annexing the territory of that Republic to the United States, and the hope and belief entertained by the Executive that the treaty with Texas for that purpose would be speedily approved and ratified by the Senate, it was regarded by the Executive to have become emphatically its duty to concentrate in the Gulf of Mexico and its vicinity, as a precautionary measure, as large a portion of the home squadron, under the command of Captain Conner, as could well be drawn together, and at the same time to assemble at Fort Jesup, on the borders of Texas, as large a military force as the demands of the service at other encampments would authorize to be detached. For the number of ships already in the Gulf and the waters contiguous thereto and such as are placed under orders for that destination, and of troops now assembled upon the frontier, I refer you to the accompanying reports from the Secretaries of the War and Navy Departments. It will also be perceived by the Senate, by referring to the orders of the Navy Department which are herewith transmitted, that the naval officer in command of the fleet is directed to cause his ships to perform all the duties of a fleet of observation and to apprise the Executive of any indication of a hostile design upon Texas on the part of any nation pending the deliberations of the Senate upon the treaty, with a view that the same should promptly be submitted to Congress for its mature deliberation. At the same time, it is due to myself that I should declare it as my opinion that the United States having by the treaty of annexation acquired a title to Texas which requires only the action of the Senate to perfect it, no other power could be permitted to invade and by force of arms to possess itself of any portion of the territory of Texas pending your deliberations upon the treaty without placing itself in an hostile attitude to the United States and justifying the employment of any military means at our disposal to drive back the invasion. At the same time, it is my opinion that Mexico or any other power will find in your approval of the treaty no just cause of war against the United States, nor do I believe that there is any serious hazard of war to be found in the fact of such approval. Nevertheless, every proper measure will be resorted to by the Executive to preserve upon an honorable and just basis the public peace by reconciling Mexico, through a liberal course of policy, to to the treaty.

* * * *

and

In answer to the resolution of the Senate of the 13th instant, requesting to be informed "whether a messenger has been sent to Mexico with a view to obtain her consent to the treaty with Texas, and, if so, to communicate to the Senate a copy of the dispatches of which he is bearer and a copy of the instructions given to said messenger; and also to inform the Senate within what time said messenger is expected to return," I have to say that no messenger has been sent to Mexico in order to obtain her assent to the treaty with Texas, it not being regarded by the Executive as in any degree requisite to obtain such consent in order (should the Senate ratify the treaty) to perfect the title of the United States to the territory thus acquired, the title to the same being full and perfect without the assent of any third power. The Executive has negotiated with Texas as an independent power of the world, long since recognized as such by the United States and other powers, and as subordinate in all her rights of full sovereignty to no other power. A messenger has been dispatched to our minister at Mexico as bearer of the dispatch already communicated to the Senate, and which is to be found in the letter addressed to Mr. Green, and forms a part of the documents ordered confidentially to be printed for the use of the Senate. That dispatch was dictated by a desire to preserve the peace of the two countries by denying to Mexico all pretext for assuming a belligerent attitude to the United States as she had threatened to do, in the event of the annexation of Texas to the United States, by the dispatch of her Government which was communicated by me to Congress at the opening of its present session. The messenger is expected to return before the 15th of June next, but he may be detained to a later day. The recently appointed envoy from the United States to Mexico will be sent so soon as the final action is had on the question of annexation, at which time, and not before, can his instructions be understandingly prepared.

JOHN TYLER

FOURTH ANNUAL MESSAGE
December 3, 1844

*When the senate turned down the treaty for annexation of
Texas Tyler, intent upon it as the great achievement of
his administration, sought other ways of accomplishing
the same end. On June 10, 1844, he sent a lengthy message to the House of Representatives. It contained copies
of all the correspondence and documents submitted to the
Senate to support the treaty and called upon the House to
begin the actions necessary to bring about annexation.*

*In this Fourth annual message Tyler summarized the ar-
guments and pointed to the results of the election of
1844, in which expansionist Polk, with Tyler's support,
had defeated the Whig Clay, as evidence of the people's
desire for Congress to act.*

*He then turned to domestic affairs and painted a picture
of the nation's financial condition that was in happy contrast with the situation which had prevailed at the beginning of his administration.*

In my last annual message I felt it to be my duty to make known to
Congress, in terms both plain and emphatic, my opinion in regard to
the war which has so long existed between Mexico and Texas, which
since the battle of San Jacinto has consisted altogether of predatory
incursions, attended by circumstances revolting to humanity. I repeat
now what I then said, that after eight years of feeble and ineffectual
efforts to reconquer Texas it was time that the war should have
ceased. The United States have a direct interest in the question. The
contiguity of the two nations to our territory was but too well calculated to involve our peace. Unjust suspicions were engendered in the
mind of one or the other of the belligerents against us, and as a
necessary consequence American interests were made to suffer and
our peace became daily endangered; in addition to which it must have
been obvious to all that the exhaustion produced by the war subjected
both Mexico and Texas to the interference of other powers, which,
without the interposition of this Government, might eventuate in the
most serious injury to the United States. This Government from time
to time exerted its friendly offices to bring about a termination of
hostilities upon terms honorable alike to both the belligerents. Its
efforts in this behalf proved unavailing. Mexico seemed almost without an object to persevere in the war, and no other alternative was
left the Executive but to take advantage of the well-known dispostions
of Texas and to invite her to enter into a treaty for annexing her
territory to that of the United States.

Since your last session Mexico has threatened to renew the war, and has either made or proposes to make formidable preparations for invading Texas. She has issued decrees and proclamations, preparatory to the commencement of hostilities, full of threats revolting to humanity, and which if carried into effect would arouse the attention of all Christendom. This new demonstration of feeling, there is too much reason to believe, has been produced in consequence of the negotiation of the late treaty of annexation with Texas. The Executive, therefore, could not be indifferent to such proceedings, and it felt it to be due as well to itself as to the honor of the country that a strong representation should be made to the Mexican Government upon the subject. This was accordingly done, as will be seen by the copy of the accompanying dispatch from the Secretary of State to the United States envoy at Mexico. Mexico has no right to jeopard the peace of the world by urging any longer a useless and fruitless contest. Such a condition of things would not be tolerated on the European continent. Why should it be on this? A war of desolation, such as is now threatened by Mexico, can not be waged without involving our peace and tranquility. It is idle to believe that such a war could be looked upon with indifference by our own citizens inhabiting adjoining States; and our neutrality would be violated in despite of all efforts on the part of the Government to prevent it. The country is settled by emigrants from the United States under invitations held out to them by Spain and Mexico. These emigrants have left behind them friends and relatives, who would not fail to sympathize with them in their difficulties, and who would be led by those sympathies to participate in their struggles, however energetic the action of the Government to prevent it. Nor would the numerous and formidable bands of Indians – the most warlike to be found in any land - which occupy the the extensive regions contiguous to the States of Arkansas and Missouri, and who are in possession of large tracts of country within the limits of Texas, be likely to remain passive. The inclinations of those numerous tribes lead them invariably to war whenever pretexts exist.

Mexico had no just ground of displeasure against this Government or people for negotiating the treaty. What interest of hers was affected by the treaty? She was despoiled of nothing, since Texas was forever lost to her. The independence of Texas was recognized by several of the leading powers of the earth. She was free to treat, free to adopt her own line of policy, free to take the course which she believed was best calculated to secure her happiness.

Her Government and people decided on annexation to the United States, and the Executive saw in the acquisition of such a territory the means of advancing their permanent happiness and glory. What principle of good faith, then, was violated? What rule of political morals trampled under foot? So far as Mexico herself was concerned, the measure should have been regarded by her as highly beneficial.

Her inability to reconquer Texas had been exhibited, I repeat, by eight (now nine) years of fruitless and ruinous contest. In the meantime Texas has been growing in population and resources. Emigration has flowed into her territory from all parts of the world in a current which continues to increase in strength. Mexico requires a permanent boundary between that young Repbulic and herself. Texas at no distant day, if she continues separate and detached from the United States, will inevitably seek to consolidate her strength by adding to her domain the contiguous Provinces of Mexico. The spirit of revolt from the control of the central Government has heretofore manifested itself in some of those Provinces, and it is fair to infer that they would be inclined to take the first favorable opportunity to proclaim their independence and to form close alliances with Texas. The war would thus be endless, or if cessations of hostilities should occur they would only endur for a season. The interests of Mexico, therefore, could in nothing be better consulted than in a peace with her neighbors which would result in the establishment of apermanent boundary. Upon the ratification of the treaty the Executive was prepared to treat with her on the most liberal basis. Hence the boundaries of Texas were left undefined by the treaty. The Executive proposed to settle these upon terms that all the world should have pronounced just and reasonable. No negotiation upon that point could have been undertaken between the United States and Mexico in advance of the ratification of the treaty. We should have had no right, no power, no authority, to have conducted such a negotiation, and to have undertaken it would have been an assumption equally revolting to the pride of Mexico and Texas and subjecting us to the charge of arrogance, while to have proposed in advance of annexation to satisfy Mexico for any contingent interest she might have in Texas would have been to have treated Texas not as an independent power, but as a mere dependency of Mexico. This assumption could not have been acted on by the Executive without setting at defiance your own solemn declaration that that Republic was an independent State. Mexico had, it is true, threatened war against the United States in the event the treaty of annexation was ratified. The Executive could not permit itself to be influenced by this threat. It represented in this the spirit of our people, who are ready to sacrifce much for peace, but nothing to intimidation. A war under any circumstances is greatly to be deplored, and the United States is the last nation to desire it; but if, as the condition of peace, it be required of us to forego the unquestionable right of treating with an independent power of our own continent upon matters highly interesting to both, and that upon a naked and unsustained pretension of claim by a third power to control the free will of the power with whom we treat, devoted as we may be to peace and anxious to cultivate friendly relations with the whole world, the Executive does not hesitate to say that the people of the United States would be ready to brave all consequences sooner than submit to such condition. But no apprehension of war was entertained by the Executive, and I must express frankly the opinion that had the treaty been ratified by the Senate it would have been followed by a prompt settlement, to the entire satisfaction of Mexico, of every matter in difference between the two countries. Seeing, then, that new preparations for hostile invasion of Texas were about to be adopted by Mexico, and that these were brought about because Texas had adopted the suggestions of the Executive upon the subject of annexation, it could not passively have folded its arms and permitted a war, threatened to be accompanied by every act that could mark a barbarous age, to be waged against her because she had done so.

Other considerations of a controlling character influenced the course of the Executive. The treaty which had thus been negotiated had failed to receive the ratification of the Senate. One of the chief objections which was urged against it was found to consist in the fact that the question of annexation had not been submitted to the ordeal of public opinion in the United States. However untenable such an objection was esteemed to be, in view of the unquestionable power of the Executive to negotiate the treaty and the great and lasting interest involved in the question, I felt it to be my duty to submit the whole subject to Congress as the best expounders of popular sentiment. No definitive action having been taken on the subject by Congress, the question referred itself directly to the decision of the States and people. The great popular election which has just terminated afforded the best opportunity of ascertaining the will of the States and the people upon it. Pending that issue it became the imperative duty of the Executive to inform Mexico that the question of annexation was still before the American people, and that until their decision was pronounced any serious invasion of Texas would be regarded as an attempt to forestall their judgment and could not be looked upon with indifference. I am most happy to inform you that no such invasion has taken place; and I trust that whatever your action may be upon it Mexico will see the importance of deciding the matter by a resort to peaceful expedients in preference to those of arms. The decision of the people and the States on this great and interesting subject has been decisively manifested. The question of annexation has been presented nakedly to their consideration. By the treaty itself all collateral and incidental issues which were calculated to divide and distract the public councils were carefully avoided. These were left to the wisdom of the future to determine. It presented, I repeat, the isolated question of annexation, and in that form it has been submitted to the ordeal of public sentiment. A controlling majority of the people and a large majority of the States have declared in favor of immediate annexation. Instructions have thus come up to both branches of Congress from their respective constituents in terms the most emphatic. It is the will of both the people and the States that Texas shall be annexed to the Union promptly and immediately. It may be hoped that in carrying into execution the public will thus declared all collateral issues may be avoided. Future Legislatures can best decide as to the number of States which should be formed out of the territory when the time has arrived for deciding that question. So with all others. By the treaty the United States assumed the payment of the debts of Texas to an amount not exceeding $10,000,000, to be paid, with the exception of a sum falling short of $400,000, exclusively out of the proceeds of the sales of her public lands. We could not with honor take the lands without assuming the full payment of all incumbrances upon them.

Nothing has occurred since your last session to induce a doubt that the dispositions of Texas remain unaltered. No intimation of an altered determination on the part of her Government and people has been furnished to the Executive. She still desires to throw herself under the protection of our laws and to partake of the blessings of our federative system, while every American interest would seem to require it. The extension of our coastwise and foreign trade to an amount almost incalculable, the enlargement of the market for our manufactures, a constantly growing market for our agricultural productions, safety to our frontiers, and additional strength and stability to the Union-these are the results which would rapidly develop themselves upon the consummation of the measure of annexation. In such event I will not doubt but that Mexico would find her true interest to consist in meeting the advances of this Government in a spirit of amity. Nor do I apprehend any serious complaint from any other quarter; no sufficient ground exists for such complaint. We should interfere in no respect with the rights of any other nation. There can not be gathered from the act any design on our part to do so with their possessions on this continent. We have interposed no impediments in the way of such acquisitions of territory, large and extensive as many of them are, as the leading powers of Europe have made from time to time in every part of the world. We seek no conquest made by war. No intrigue will have been resorted to or acts of diplomacy essayed to accomplish the annexation of Texas. Free and independent herself, she asks to be received into our Union. It is a question for our own decision whether she shall be received or not.

The two Governments having already agreed through their respective organs on the terms of annexation, I would recommend their adoption by Congress in the form of a joint resolution or act to be perfected and made binding on the two countries when adopted in like manner by the Government of Texas.

In order that the subject may be fully presented in all its bearings, the correspondence which has taken place in reference to it since the adjournment of Congress between the United States, Texas, and Mexico is here with transmitted.

The amendments proposed by the Senate to the convention concluded between the United States and Mexico on the 20th of November, 1843, have been transmitted through our minister for the concurrence of the Mexican Government, but, although urged thereto, no action has yet been had on the subject, nor has any answer been given which would authorize a favorable conclusion in the future.

The decrees of September, 1843, in relation to the retail trade, the order for the expulsion of foreigners, and that of a more recent date in regard to passports — all which are considered as in violation of the treaty of amity and commerce between the two countries — have led to a correspondence of considerable length between the minister for foreign relations and our representatives at Mexico, but without any satisfactory result. They remain still unadjusted, and many and serious inconveniences have already resulted to our citizens in consequence of them.

Questions growing out of the act of disarming a body of Texan troops under the command of Major Snively by an officer in the service of the United States, acting under the orders of our Government, and the forcible entry into the custom-house at Bryarlys Landing, on Red River, by certain citizens of the United States, and taking away therefrom the goods seized by the collector of the customs as forfeited under the laws of Texas, have been adjusted so far as the powers of the Executive extend. The correspondence between the two Governments in reference to both subjects will be found amongst the accompanying documents. It contains a full statement of all the facts and circumstances, with the views taken on both sides and the principles on which the questions have been adjusted. It remains for Congress to make the necessary appropriation to carry the arrangement into effect, which I respectfully recommend.

The greatly improved condition of the Treasury affords a subject for general congratulation. The paralysis which had fallen on trade and commerce, and which subjected the Government to the necessity of resorting to loans and the issue of Treasury notes to a large amount, has passed away, and after the payment of upward of $7,000,000 on account of the interest, and in redemption of more than $5,000,000 of the public debt which falls due on the 1st of January next, and setting apart upward of $2,000,000 for the payment of outstanding Treasury notes and meeting an installment of the debts of the corporate cities of the District of Columbia, an estimated surplus of upward of $7,000,000 over and above the existing appropriations will remain in the Treasury at the close of the fiscal year. Should the Treasury notes continue outstanding as heretofore, that surplus will be considerably augmented. Although all interest has ceased upon them and the Government has invited their return to the Treasury, yet they remain outstanding, affording great facilities to commerce, and establishing the fact that under a well-regulated system of finance the Government has resources within itself which render it independent in time of need, not only of private loans, but also of bank facilities.

The only remaining subject of regret is that the remaining stocks of the Government do not fall due at an earlier day, since their redemption would be entirely within its control. As it is, it may be well worthy the consideration of Congress whether the law establishing the sinking fund (under the operation of which the debts of the Revolution and last war with Great Britain were to a great extent extinguished) should not, with proper modifications, so as to prevent an accumulation of surpluses, and limited in amount to a specific sum, be reenacted. Such provision, which would authorize the Government to go into the market for a purchase of its own stock on fair terms, would serve to maintain its credit at the highest point and prevent to a great extent those fluctuations in the price of its securities which might under other circumstances affect its credit. No apprehension of this sort is at this moment entertained, since the stocks of the Government, which but two years ago were offered for sale to capitalists at home and abroad at a depreciation, and could find no purchasers, are now greatly above par in the hands of the holders; but a wise and prudent forecast admonishes us to place beyond the reach of contingency the public credit.

It must also be a matter of unmingled gratification that under the existing financial system (resting upon the act of 1789 and the resolution of 1816) the currency of the country has attained a state of perfect soundness; and the rates of exchange between different parts of the Union, which in 1841 denoted by their enormous amount the great depreciation and, in fact, worthlessness of the currency in most of the States, are now reduced to little more than the mere expense of transporting specie from place to place and the risk incident to the operation. In a new country like that of the United States, where so many inducements are held out for speculation, the depositories of the surplus revenue, consisting of banks of any description, when it reaches any considerable amount, require the closest vigilance on the part of the Government. All banking institutions, under whatever denomination they may pass, are governed by an almost exclusive regard to the interest of the stockholders. That interest consists in the augmentation of profits in the form of dividends, and a large surplus revenue intrusted to their custody is but too apt to lead to excessive loans and to extravagantly large issue of paper. As a necessary consequence prices are nominally increased and the speculative mania very soon seizes upon the public mind. A fictitious state of prosperity for a season exists, and, in the language of the day, money becomes plenty. Contracts are entered into by individuals resting on this unsubstanial state of things, but the delusion speedily passes away and the country is overrun with an indebtedness so weighty as to overwhelm many and to visit every department of industry with great and ruinous embarrassment. The greatest vigilance becomes necessary on the part of Government to guard against this state of things. The depositories must be given distinctly to understand that the favors of the Government will be altogether withdrawn, or substantially diminished, if its revenues shall be regarded as additions to their banking capital or as the foundation of an enlarged circulation.

The Government, through its revenue, has at all times an important part to perform in connection with the currency, and its greatly depends upon its vigilance and care whether the country be involved in embarrassments similar to those which it has had recently to encounter, or, aided by the action of the Treasury, shall be preserved in a sound and healthy condition.

The dangers to be guarded against are greatly augmented by too large a surplus of revenue. When that surplus greatly exceeds in amount what shall be required by a wise and prudent forecast to meet unforeseen contingencies, the Legislature itself may come to be seized with a disposition to indulge in extravagant appropriation to objects many of which may, and most probably would, be found to conflict with the Constitution. A fancied expediency is elevated above constitutional authority, and a reckless and wasteful extravagance but too certainly follows.

SUBMISSION OF TREATY WITH CHINA
January 22, 1845

*The British victory over China in the Opium War opened
that empire to trade and relations with the western nations. The United States was one of the first to follow
England's example and negotiate a treaty. The negotiation of the treaty had been considered important enough
for Tyler to hope that Edward Everett, minister to Great
Britain, would accept it thus opening up the post in London for Webster and the Secretaryship of State for Upshur.
Everett, however declined and Caleb Cushing undertook
the mission.*

*Submitting the ratified treaty to Congress, Tyler called
for the establishment of full diplomatic relations with
China.*

To the Senate and House of Representatives of the United States:

I communicate herewith an abstract of the treaty between the
United States of America and the Chinese Empire concluded at Wang-
Hiya on the 3d of July last, and ratified by the Senate on the 16th instant, and which, having also been ratified by the Emperor of China,
now awaits only the exchange of the ratifications in China, from which
it will be seen that the special mission authorized by Congress for
this purpose has fully succeeded in the accomplishment so far of the
great objects for which it was appointed, and in placing our relations
with China on a new footing eminently favorable to the commerce and
other interests of the United States.

In view of the magnitude and importance of our national concerns,
actual and prospective, in China, I submit to the consideration of Congress the expediency of providing for the preservation and cultivation
of the subsisting relations of amity between the United States and the
Chinese Government, either by means of a permanent minister or
commissioner with diplomatic functions, as in the case of certain of
the Mohammedan States. It appears by one of the extracts annexed that
the establishment of the British Government in China consists both of
a plenipotentiary and also of paid consuls for all the five ports, one of
whom has the title and exercises the functions of consul-general; and
France has also a salaried consul-general, and the interests of the

United States seem in like manner to call for some representative in China of a higher class than an ordinary commercial consulate.

I also submit to the consideration of Congress the expediency of making some special provision by law for the security of the independent and honorable position which the treaty of Wang-Hiya confers on citizens of the United States residing or doing business in China. By the twenty-first and twenty-fifth articles of the treaty (copies of which are subjoined in extenso) citizens of the United States in China are wholly exempted, as well in criminal as in civil matters, from the local juridsdiction of the Chinese Government and made amenable to the laws and subject to the jurisdiction of the appropriate authorities of the United States alone. Some action on the part of Congress seems desirable in order to give full effect to these important concessions of the Chinese Government.

                                                    JOHN TYLER

BIBLIOGRAPHICAL AIDS

The works cited below are some of the more important ones which shed light on John Tyler, his times, and on the institution of the Presidency. Emphasis has been placed on the period that he was in office and on works that are recent and accessible. Additional titles may be found in And Tyler Too and John Tyler, Champion of the Old South (see Biographies below), A Bibliography of William Henry Harrison, John Tyler, James Polk, compiled by John W. Cronin and W. Harvey Wise (Washington, 1935), The Encyclopedia of American History, revised edition, edited by Richard B. Morris (New York, 1965), the Harvard Guide to American History and the American Historical Association's Guide to Historical Literature. Additional essays can be found through the Reader's Guide to Periodical Literature and the Social Science and Humanities Index.

An asterisk identifies a book that is currently available in paperback.

SOURCE MATERIALS

The primary collection of Tyler manuscript materials, including reflections on social life and customs as well as political correspondence, is in the Library of Congress. Three reels of material are available on microfilm in the Presidential Papers Microfilm series. There is an additional collection at the West Virginia University Library which contains the materials gathered by Chitwood in preparing his biography. Additional sources, scattered among various collections, can be located through The National Union Catalog of Manuscript Collections. The most valuable published source of materials is Lyon Gardiner Tyler's Letters. Published sources include:

Reese, George H. Proceedings of the Virginia State Convention of 1861, February 13-May 1. Richmond.

Richardson, James D. Messages and Papers of the Presidents, 1789-1897. Vol. IV. Washington, 1897.

Tyler, Lyon Gardiner. The Letters and Times of the Tylers. 3 vols. Richmond, 1884-1896.

BIOGRAPHIES

There have been two twentieth century biographies of Tyler, those of Chitwood and Seager, but the definitive work is clearly yet to be written. Chitwood acts too much as the champion of his "Champion of the Old South" while Seager is most careful when dealing with matters of social life and customs. On many issues, the reader must go back to the family biography of Lyon Gardiner Tyler and examine the sources.

Chitwood, Oliver Perry. John Tyler, Champion of the Old South. New York, 1939. Reprinted in 1964, the volume is readily available. Using family materials not available to earlier researchers, Chitwood prepared a very favorable biography.

Seager, Robert II. and Tyler too: A Biography of John and Julia Gardiner Tyler. New York, 1963. This is labelled as a biography of two people, John and Julia Gardiner Tyler. It might even be more correct to say that it is of one person, Tyler, and a family, the Gardiners. It is interestingly written and presents fascinating insight into the extent to which prominent people, dealing with national crises, can still be most concerned about their social positions. It does not, however, do justice to the political crises of the Tyler administration. To be fair to the author, it should be noted that it was not intended to.

Tyler, Lyon Gardiner. The Letters and Times of the Tylers. 3 vols. Richmond, 1884-1896. A biography of Judge John Tyler (1747-1813) and his son President Tyler built around hundreds of letters and other documents. It is a filial work and must be read as such, but, because of the documents, is still a very valuable one.

ESSAYS

There are several good articles on Tyler in the enclyclopedias and collections. The best are those by Thomas P. Abernathy in the Dictionary of American Biography, Fletcher M. Green in the Encyclopaedia Britannica and George E. Mowry in Colliers Enclyclopedia. Other essays of interest are:

Jeffries, Ona Griffin. "Southern Hospitality, The John Tylers," In and Out of the White House...from Washington to the Eisenhowers, New York, 1960. Popularly written but of interest because of the importance of social life in the Tyler administration. Seager provides a much fuller and more scholarly discussion but this provides a brief survey or the highlights.

Krueger, David W. "The Clay-Tyler Feud, 1841-1842," The Filson Club History Quarterly, XLII (April, 1968), 162-175. Sees cause of break over the bank bills to be Clay's concern that Tyler's succession had cancelled Harrison's guarantee of an open field for the presidency in 1844, Tyler's concern for states' rights, and the failure of each to recognize that what was uppermost in his own mind was not uppermost in the other's mind.

Martin, Asa E. "The 'Rebel' at Sherwood Forest," After the White House, State College, Pa., 1951.

Timberlake, Richard H., Jr. "The Specie Circular and the Distribution of the Surplus," Journal of Political Economy, LXVIII (April, 1960), 109-117. While not directly about Tyler, it is of interest because of the way in which the economy recovered in spite of the failure of Tyler and Congress to agree on any actions. Timberlake argues that, at least at that time, government actions had little affect on the overall economy.

MONOGRAPHS AND SPECIAL AREAS

Knoles, George H., ed. The Crisis of the Union. Baton Rouge, La., 1965.

Lambert, Oscar Doane. Presidential Politics in the United States 1841-1844. Durham, N.C., 1936. Concentrates on the political "in-fighting" of the period and emphasizes the extent to which the ambitions of individual leaders determined the course of the government.

Morgan, Robert J. A Whig Embattled: The Presidency under John Tyler. Lincoln, Neb., 1954.

Poage, George Rawlings. Henry Clay and the Whig Party. Chapel Hill, N.C., 1936. The Tyler administration as seen from the vantage point of Clay and his supporters.

Reeves, Jesse S. American Diplomacy under Tyler and Polk. Glou-
        cester, Mass., 1967. A reprint of the 1906 Albert Shaw Lec-
        tures on Diplomatic History.

THE PERIOD

Since the dominant political figures of the time were not the ones
elected president in the period following Jackson, a number of their
biographies are included here as an aid in developing understanding
as to why the country, the government, and the presidency was as it
was during the the Harrison-Tyler administration.

Bemis, Samuel F. John Quincy Adams and the Union. New York, 1956.

Coit, Margaret L. John C. Calhoun. Boston, 1950.*

Current, Richard N. Daniel Webster and the Rise of National Conserva-
        tism. Boston, 1955.*

Eaton, Clement. Henry Clay and the Art of American Politics. Boston
        1957.

Govan, Thomas Payne. Nicholas Biddle: Nationalist and Public Banker.
        Chicago, 1959.

Hammond, Bray. Banks and Politics in America from the Revolution
        to the Civil War. Princeton, N.J., 1957.*

McCormick, Richard P. The Second American Party System: Party
        Formation in the Jacksonian Era. Chapel Hill, N.C., 1966.*

Merk, Frederick. Manifest Destiny and Mission in American His-
        tory. New York, 1963.

Meyers, Marvin. The Jacksonian Persuasion: Politics and Belief.
        Palo Alto, Cal., 1957.*

Nichols, Roy F. The Disruption of American Democracy. New York,
        1948.

Remini, Robert V. Andrew Jackson and the Bank War. New York, 1967.*

Remini, Robert V. Martin Van Buren and the Making of the Democratic
        Party. New York, 1959.

Schlesinger, Arthur M., Jr. The Age of Jackson, Boston, 1946.*

Sellers, Charles G. James K. Polk, Jacksonian. New York, 1957.

Smith, Justin H. The Annexation of Texas. New York, 1941.

Tocqueville, Alexis de. Democracy in America. New York, 1954.*

Van Deusen, Glyndon G. The Jacksonian Era: 1828-1848. New York, 1959.*

Van Deusen, Glyndon G. Thurlow Weed, Wizard of the Lobby. Boston, 1947.

Wiltse, Charles M. John C. Calhoun. 3 vols. Indianapolis, 1944-1951.

Woodford, John B. Lewis Cass, the Last Jeffersonian. New Brunswick, N.J., 1950

THE PRESIDENCY

Bailey, Thomas A. Presidential Greatness, the Image and the Man from George Washington to the Present. New York, 1966.* Tyler is given "at least a low average" grade as an able administrator with some solid accomplishments in spite of being a man without a party.

Binkley, Wilfred E. The Man in the White House: His Powers and Duties. New York, 1964.& Both highly readable and informative.

Binkley, Wilfred E. President and Congress. 3rd revised edition. New York, 1967.*

Brown, Stuart Gerry. The American Presidency: Leadership, Partisanship and Popularity. New York, 1966.* An exploration into the sources and uses of presidential poularity.

Corwin, Edward S. The President: Office and Powers. 4th edition. New York, 1957.* The standard work on the presidency by an authority on the Constitution. Focuses on the office as created in that document and shows how specific powers have been added, extended and changed over the years.

Cunliffe, Marcus et al. The American Heritage History of the Presidency. New York, 1968. Highly readable and copiously illustrated.

Hamilton, Holman. White House Images and Realities. Gainesville, Fla., 1958. A short study of the backgrounds and images necessary to gain nomination, election and a good historical reputation.

Heller, Francis H. The Presidency: A Modern Perspective. New York, 1960.* Considers the need for modern scientific management techniques and organization in the institution.

Kane, Joseph Nathan. Facts about the Presidents. Revised ed. New York, 1968.*

Koenig, Louis W. The Chief Executive. Revised ed. New York, 1968.

Koenig, Louis W. Official Makers of Public Policy: Congress and the President. Glenview, Ill., 1967.*

Laski, Harold J. The American Presidency. New York, 1940.*

Neustadt, Richard E. Presidential Power. New York, 1964.* An important analysis of the actual power of the office noting the limitlessness of this power in some areas and its definite limits in others.

Rossiter, Clinton. The American Presidency. 2nd ed. New York, 1960.*

Young, Donald. American Roulette, The History and Dilemma of the Vice Presidency. New York, 1965.

NAME INDEX

143

TITLES IN THE OCEANA PRESIDENTIAL CHRONOLOGY SERIES

Reference books containing
Chronology—Documents—Bibliographical Aids
for each President covered.
Series Editor: **Howard F. Bremer**

GEORGE WASHINGTON*
edited by Howard F. Bremer
JOHN ADAMS*
edited by Howard F. Bremer
JAMES BUCHANAN*
edited by Irving J. Sloan
GROVER CLEVELAND**
edited by Robert I. Vexler
FRANKLIN PIERCE*
edited by Irving J. Sloan
ULYSSES S. GRANT**
edited by Philip R. Moran
MARTIN VAN BUREN**
edited by Irving J. Sloan
THEODORE ROOSEVELT**
edited by Gilbert Black
BENJAMIN HARRISON*
edited by Harry J. Sievers
JAMES MONROE*
edited by Ian Elliot
WOODROW WILSON**
edited by Robert I. Vexler
RUTHERFORD B. HAYES*
edited by Arthur Bishop
ANDREW JACKSON**
edited by Ronald Shaw
JAMES MADISON**
edited by Ian Elliot
HARRY S TRUMAN***
edited by Howard B. Furer
WARREN HARDING**
edited by Philip Moran
DWIGHT D. EISENHOWER***
edited by Robert I. Vexler
JAMES K. POLK*
edited by John J. Farrell

JOHN QUINCY ADAMS*
edited by Kenneth Jones
HARRISON/TYLER***
edited by David A. Durfee
ABRAHAM LINCOLN***
edited by Ian Elliot
GARFIELD/ARTHUR***
edited by Howard B. Furer
Available Soon
WILLIAM McKINLEY
edited by Harry J. Sievers
ANDREW JOHNSON
edited by John N. Dickinson
WILLIAM HOWARD TAFT
edited by Gilbert Black
JOHN F. KENNEDY
edited by Ralph A. Stone
THOMAS JEFFERSON
edited by Arthur Bishop
TAYLOR/FILLMORE
edited by John J. Farrell
CALVIN COOLIDGE
edited by Philip Moran
LYNDON B. JOHNSON
edited by Howard B. Furer
FRANKLIN D. ROOSEVELT
edited by Howard F. Bremer
HERBERT HOOVER
edited by Arnold Rice

*   96 pages, $3.00/B
** 128 pages, $4.00/B
*** 160 pages, $5.00/B